Jeff Galloway

Running Until You're 100

Meyer & Meyer Sport

British Library Cataloguing in Publication Data
A catalogue record for this book is available from the British Library

Jeff Galloway: Running until you're 100
Maidenhead: Meyer & Meyer Sport (UK) Ltd., 2007
ISBN: 978-1-84126-309-0

© 2007 by Meyer & Meyer Sport (UK) Ltd.
3rd Edition, 2010
Aachen, Adelaide, Auckland, Budapest, Cape Town, Graz, Indianapolis,
Maidenhead, New York, Olten (CH), Singapore, Toronto
 Member of the World
Sport Publishers' Association (WSPA)
www.w-s-p-a.org
Printed and bound by: B.O.S.S Druck und Medien GmbH, Germany
ISBN: 978-1-84126-309-0
E-Mail: info@m-m-sports.com
www.m-m-sports.com

Jeff Galloway
RUNNING UNTIL YOU'RE 100

CONTENTS

Dedication

At the age of 81, Kitty entered the Peachtree (10K) road race. One year before, she finished with no major problems, but things had changed. Though she never smoked, a tumor was discovered in the sensitive bronchial passages near her heart—and was inoperable.

While her doctor was OK with her decision to race, I asked her several times whether she should challenge herself on a hilly 6 mile course in hot Atlanta Ga., on July 4th. She didn't argue with me, but in her quiet way, I could tell that my questions only magnified her determination. One of the primary reasons, however, may be the result of having grown up during the great depression. She couldn't get a refund on the entry fee, and was determined to get her money's worth.

I believe that Kitty would have had no major problems if the temperature had remained as it was at the start—60 degrees Fahrenheit. Unfortunately, she was in the last group starting much later, and the temperature increased every few minutes. She knew she was in trouble at 3 miles (over 80°F with high humidity) but struggled up Cardiac hill past the 4 mile mark when there seemed to be nothing left in the tank.

A few minutes later, the City of Atlanta street sweeper approached. Most Peachtree participants know and fear the "grim sweeper" because when it catches you, your race is over. Kitty didn't care because she had been physically spent for 30 minutes.

This time, the sweeper stopped. Kitty motioned for the driver to move on. He stuck his head out the window and told her that she was just as important as any other runner in the race, and that he was going to stay behind her until she finished. That's all she needed. It was a real struggle but you wouldn't have known it as she somehow found a spring in her step, crossing the 6.2 mile mark with her head held high.

Kitty Galloway taught me, by example, the principles that are the foundation of my life: never give up, take control over each day, confront every challenge and do your best. She crossed her final finish line about 18 months after her last Peachtree—mentally sharp, with her head held high. She was my Mom and my hero.

How Active Do You Want to Be?

I believe that when running is balanced with rest it...

- Delivers the best attitude boost you can get
- Produces enhanced vitality that lasts all day
- Is the best stress reducer
- Bestows a significant sense of achievement
- Raises your body's physical performance capability
- Blends body, mind and spirit better than any activity
- Bestows benefits that improve life in many unique ways

If exercise were a controlled medication, it would be the most heavily prescribed on record. If running were a drug to combat depression and increase vitality, it would be a blockbuster. The benefits from exercise are almost limitless, and there seems to be no activity that maximizes these than does running.

Running stimulates your body to improve overall physical and mental capacity. Research indicates that significant exertion each week can extend the length of your life. The increased endurance and physical capacity gained from years of running results in a more active lifestyle to the end of your days.

By balancing stress and rest, walking and running, nutrition and exercise, everyone can gain a great deal of control over how much vitality will be experienced later in life. The purpose of this book is not merely to help you move down the road or trail until you're 100. Inside, you'll also find practical tips about how to make adjustments so that you can enjoy every run.

In the next few chapters, you'll see what the research says about running and the aging process—lots of good news. While it's a fact that our body resources are reduced year by year, I've heard from thousands of runners who've added more rest and inserted more frequent walk breaks into their runs. The results are almost magical: a high quality of running and life into their 60s, 70s and 80s.

We don't know the year we will leave this earth. But, if you mentally project yourself running until the century mark, and make the right adjustments, you'll expect and achieve more vitality during every decade of your life. Positive mental visions, with the use of the tools below, can give you a major amount of control over your energy and health.

In the next chapter, you'll read about some inspiring individuals who've confronted the never-ending challenges of living and exercising past the age of 70, 80, and 90. There is something in the human spirit that is positively engaged by good examples, and you'll find more at the finish line of practically every running event.

If there's one training component in the book that helps more than any other it is my run-walk-run™ method. I've now heard from thousands of the "over 50" crowd who've returned to enjoyable running by using this method. Some have improved their finish times significantly by inserting walk breaks. There's no doubt that this method prolongs your running life.

There are many suggestions in this book that have helped thousands to experience the joy and sense of freedom that only running delivers into the latter stages of life. I want you to take control of your running enjoyment and fatigue while staying injury free. I offer this advice after working with more than 200,000 runners, over more than 30 years of coaching. So lace up your running shoes and join the growing number of runners past the age of 60, 80 and beyond who enjoy running as much as those in their 20s.

If You Don't Give Up ....You Win!

A few years ago, I met a 93-year-old runner who ran in the popular Crim 10 mile race in Flint, Mich. He was just as excited about the race as the 20 year olds, and more mentally sharp than some of the younger runners as he talked about it. A recent news clipping showed a 101-year-old man running in a veteran's track meet. He set a world record. In fact, there are many opportunities for setting records if you'll keep running until 100.

Unfortunately many people over the age of 50 believe that they cannot, or should not, increase their level of exercise. A high percentage believes that it is not possible for those over 60 to go from a very sedentary lifestyle into training for a distance event. My dear mom (see the dedication of this book) initially felt this way— but turned things around and inspired me. In this chapter you'll meet some "ordinary people" who have pushed back traditional limits and expectations. They will be the first to tell you to stay in touch with your doctor from the start of the fitness journey.

Running with cancer

"If I had to choose between my old pre-cancer life as a somewhat depressed, overweight, unmotivated and unfulfilled couch potato and my current life with cancer it's easy. I'm energetic, happy, motivated and love life each day." Lee Kilpack

In 1996 Lee Kilpack was diagnosed with breast cancer, with lymph node involvement. She began a treatment plan of surgery, chemo, and radiation. Lee had never exercised. The diagnosis was a shock to her spirit, and the treatment tested body, mind and will power.

By 2000, things weren't looking very good, and she felt bad most of the time. Then, one morning, she woke up with the desire to start taking care of her body. She hired a personal trainer that day. By 2001, she was walking every day. Later that year she had inserted some running into the walks. In 2002, Lee walked the 3-Day/60 Mile Breast Cancer Walk and raised $3,000 for the cause.

The training for and the completion of such a strenuous event produced a big letdown in motivation, with extended recovery from injuries, aches and pains. Lee struggled, and finally started running regularly in December of 2003. After the '04 New Year, Lee set a bigger goal—to finish a marathon in November. The training program she chose was too adverse and she became injured in September. She didn't give up.

In early 2005, her doctor cleared her to start running again. She picked my more conservative training program. I worked with Lee via email and often found it hard to hold back her energy and drive. The training for the Marine Corps Marathon was more of a challenge than for most because she relocated to the Gulf Coast to volunteer for relief efforts for Hurricane Katrina—squeezing in long runs after exhausting days. Somehow, she also hikes, cycles, and paddles hard in her kayak; on the "off days" she doesn't run.

She regularly gets screened for tumor markers. While the tests show her out of the normal range, her doctor does not see a threat in the near future, and supports her running. "I don't know what the future holds for me. If it is metastasis tomorrow, I would be OK with that. What a good life I've been given. My health and happiness have never been better. What my oncologist doesn't understand is what a dynamite combo vitality and endorphins make."

Lee is training for 3 half marathons and 3 marathons in the next year. "I am so thankful for my cancer. My life has been changed for the better and I can't express how great I feel now. If I had to choose between my old pre-cancer life as a somewhat depressed, overweight, unmotivated and unfulfilled couch potato and my current life with cancer it's easy. I'm energetic, happy, motivated and love life each day. I love my body, my running—life itself."

A turn-around in her 50s

Over a decade ago, Cathy Troisi patiently listened through most of the sessions of a one-day running school I conducted in Boston. I noticed a change in her energy level and attentiveness when I got into the session about my run-walk-run method. Cathy had never run before, wanted to do the Boston Marathon for a charity, and thought she had waited too long to start running. Even veteran runners told her that running would hurt her joints, past the age of 50.

Walk breaks gave her hope. She called me 6 months later, gushing with the excitement of finishing her first marathon. The excitement has not gone away.

Lifestyle before running: no physical activity, ever (except gym class in high school)

First marathon: 6 hours, using a ratio of run a minute/walk a minute

12 years later: 147 marathons, 29 ultra marathons...and counting.

# of injuries in 12 years: 0

$ raised for charity in 12 years: over $70,000

Challenges:
- Caring for family
- Owner of two pre-schools
- Daughter has cancer, Cathy has cared for her and the grandkids
- Hereditary high level of cholesterol

What running has done for her:
- Appreciation of health potential, human performance potential, and to not take health for granted
- More conscious of diet
- "I've never felt my age (now, over 60)"
- Social camaraderie across 50 states
- Enriching travel experiences—shared
- Positive mental outlook and attitude especially when challenged
- Wonderful new friends
- A chance to volunteer—give back

Visions:
- Daughter Kimi free of cancer (well on her way to this)
- To show that chronological age does not have to force one to downsize physical activity
- To lower cholesterol (on her way to doing this)
- To finish the quest of running a marathon in each of the 50 states...the second time around

"Running is a panacea for a healthy life: physically, mentally, emotionally. Aging can be a healthier process due to this simple activity. It requires minimal equipment, allows time for reflection, provides an opportunity to get in touch with nature, incurs minimal cost, and breaks down age barriers." C Troisi

A faster marathon at age 62

It was a treasure for me to know the late Dr. George Sheehan as a friend. He was not only a great ambassador of running, but a fierce competitor to the end. Just before he turned 60 years old, George's marathon times were slowing down, and he made a decision to go into "semi-running-retirement." Instead of running 5 miles every day, he ran 10 miles every other day. Due to the quality rest, and his continued focus, the great Sheehan ran the fastest marathon of his life at age 62: 3 hours and 1 minute.

Marathon records after 80

Mavis Lindgren was a sickly child and a sickly adult who was advised against exercising. She almost died of a lung infection in her late 50s. During the recovery, her new young doctor had the shocking opinion that she should walk with her husband, and kept recommending an increase in the distance she covered.

Surprisingly, Mavis found enjoyment as she felt her body come alive with improved endurance. In her 60s, she took up running with husband Carl, and quickly surpassed him. Into her late 80s she was setting age group records and had not even suffered a common cold since beginning her running career.

At about the age of 85 she slipped on a cup at the 20 mile water station of the Portland (OR) Marathon. Officials helped her up and tried to take her to a medical tent. She quietly brushed them off, saying that it was a surface injury. After she finished she went to the medical tent to find that she had been running with a broken arm.

We miss Mavis, but her pleasant, positive, quiet and tough spirit lives on.

Running with only one foot

When you start feeling sorry for yourself because your feet hurt or your legs don't have the bounce of past years, think of Kelly Luckett. Kelly lost her leg at age 2, and disconnected with the thought of regular exercise or sports. As a sedentary spouse, she watched her husband become a runner, and for years participated in Atlanta's Peachtree Road Race, which had a wheel chair division. Kelly had used a prosthetic for years, but thought that regular exercise was out of her range of possibilities.

In 2003, she decided to enter the Peachtree race herself and started walking. She overcame many unique problems relating to the mechanics of the device, and made adjustments. Since the Peachtree is listed as a running race, Kelly tried to run, but could only last for 30 seconds. She gave up many times—re-starting each time.

Slowly, she made progress, adjusting the equipment, the urethane liner, and foot gear. She made it through her first Peachtree, along with 55,000 others. She couldn't imagine running much farther than 6 miles until she attended one of my one-day running schools and learned about the run-walk-run method. We stayed in touch for the next year, fine-tuning her training and her run-walk-run ratio. I have not coached an athlete with a stronger spirit.

Her first half marathon was tough and she told me that she couldn't imagine going twice that distance at any speed. Over the next 6 months, we kept adjusting the run-walk-run ratio, and Kelly finished the Country Music Marathon in 6 hours and 46 minutes. She passed a number of runners in the last 10 miles and qualified for the world's most famous race: The Boston Marathon.

Kelly was only the third female amputee to finish this premier race. Her training paid off and she improved her time by almost 20 minutes! The next challenge is a 50 miler.

Don McNelly (85 Years Young in 2006)

a. 700+ marathons
b. Weight: 210
c. Height: 6' 1/4"
d. Started running at age 48
e. First Marathon 1969—Boston
f. Over 400 marathons since turning 70
g. Completing over 25 marathons each year
h. Married for over 64 years and counting
i. "I've never been happier in my life"

Those who meet Don find that he does not act his age: "...an enormous amount of energy, clear head, speaks intellectually about all topics, and has no signs of hearing, sight or recollection problems". He started running at age 48, and ran his first marathon almost 10 years later in 1969—the last Boston Marathon that did not require time qualification.

While he runs and walks shorter distances, during marathons and ultra marathons (more frequently than every other week) he walks.

He tried to get his father to walk or run, but to no avail. His Dad had to have both hips replaced. Don believes that running too fast, or pushing beyond your limits causes joint problems. "I sure admire strong and determined competitors but I have seen too many have to quit after too few running years". Despite his size and weight, he has no significant problems.

He's run on 5 continents, in 20 countries, all states and Canadian provinces, and is looking forward to moving into the 90 + age group.

Norm Frank 74 Years Young in 2006
a. 900 marathons
b. He's still runs all of his marathons
c. Lives in Rochester NY and New Port Richey, FL
d. Current goal: to reach 1,000
e. Norm's PR in his younger days was about 3:30. He ran 30 consecutive Boston marathons
f. He completed a marathon in each of the 50 States. He's a retired lawn maintenance company owner

Wally Herman 81 Years Young in 2006
a. Approaching 700 marathons
b. Still runs his marathons
c. Lives in Ottawa, Canada, and Lake Worth FL
d. He's finished a marathon in 99 different countries
e. Observers say he can run under 5-hours on a good day

My long-term hero

Throughout my childhood, I was an overweight, sedentary kid. But like many boys, I wanted to be like my Dad, who had been an all-state football player. I tried his sport in the 8th grade, but it wasn't the right one for me. My Dad sensed that running cross country would be a better match, and he was right.

As I got in better shape through high school and college, the fat burned off my body. At the same time, my father was putting it on, and becoming more sedentary. What bothered me most was his increasingly more negative attitude. Intuitively, I knew that exercise would help him feel better. When Aerobics was published by Dr. Kenneth Cooper in 1968, I gave a copy to Dad, which he read completely in a day or so, but didn't leave his chair. I offered to walk with him around the park, in front of his office, but he complained about the complications of varicose veins and allergies, and I didn't know enough about either condition to argue with him.

It was a high school reunion, at the age of 52, which provided the wakeup call. Out of 25 boys who had been on the Moultrie High football team, 13 had died of lifestyle degenerative diseases. During the three and a half hour drive home, Elliott Galloway realized that if he didn't make some healthy behavioral changes, he would not be attending the next reunion.

The next day, he decided to run around the golf course in front of his office. Less than a football field later, his legs gave out. The feeling of defeat drove him to try for an additional telephone pole, two days later. About a year later, Elliott Galloway's name was in the finisher's list of the Peachtree Road Race 10K. Seven years later, and 55 pounds lighter, he was running marathons—including one below 3 hours. The effects of varicose veins and allergies almost went away as he got into regular running.

Having had an irregular heart rhythm for years, his doctor ordered him, at age 75, to retire from long distance racing. But he negotiated and received clearance to finish his career with the 100th running of the Boston Marathon in 1996. I was honored to be his pacer, and as we ran and walk-breaked our way from Hopkinton into Boston, we talked about the history, the marathon memories, and were energized by the crowds.

As we turned the corner and saw the finish structure, Dad took off. Once he saw the clock, he was on a mission to break a certain time barrier, which we did: 5:59:48. He told anyone who asked about the race that he would have run much faster if I hadn't slowed him down. I didn't argue.

As Dad's life clock is ticking toward the 90 year mark, he faces the daily challenges of macular degeneration and poor hearing. An even greater stress has been the loss of my dear mother, after having been married for 63 years. But practically every day, he's on a mission to see more than 10,000 steps on his counter. When things seem really tough, Dad and I hit the road, moving our legs over the same course he used when he started—one telephone pole at a time.

He is my hero. I hope I can be like him when I grow up.

What Does the Research Say?

"For every hour you exercise, you should receive two hours added to your lifespan."

The evidence is growing that running and walking will bring quality to your life, increase longevity and will not harm your joints—when done correctly. But every year I hear statements from uninformed doctors who are prejudiced against running, don't read the research, and who mistakenly maintain that humans were not designed for running. This chapter is your guide to the research, so that you can decide.

It's my opinion, and that of many medical experts, that most people will maintain their cardiovascular system better and suffer less joint damage by regularly and gently running and walking. During a clinic on his research findings(listed below), leading researcher Dr. Paffenbarger stated that for every hour you exercise, you can expect to have your life extended by 2 hours. That's a great return on investment!

But those who choose to push into speed work and run too much or too fast for their current ability can cause orthopedic problems. Because there are many individual differences, especially during the aging process, you should find the medical experts in the areas that are important to you, and stay in touch about any problems that come up. You'll find suggestions in this book about "early warning" tests that can show potential problems, and how to choose doctors who are supportive of running and exercise. Consult your medical team on all medical issues.

Humans were designed for long distance running—and walking
In the Journal Nature, November 2004, Daniel Lieberman (Harvard), and Dennis Bramble (University of Utah) state that fossil evidence shows that ancient man ran long distances. These experts and others point to the ancient bio mechanisms of the ankle, achilles, buttocks, and many other components which are running specific adaptations. According to the extensive research of these scientists and others, one can say that humans were born to run, that covering long distances was a survival activity, and that body and mind are designed to adapt to gentle and regular walking/running. Some experts believe that ancient human ancestors ran before they walked.

Older runners can improve faster than younger runners. "You can maintain a very high performance standard into the sixth or seventh decade of life", said Dr. Peter Jokl, British Journal of Sports Medicine August 2004 (reported in MSNBC.com). This study found that runners over 50 years old improved their times in the NYC Marathon more than runners in younger age groups.

Exercise Prolongs Life

Living longer is related to the number of calories burned per week. Dr. Ralph Paffenbarger conducted a highly acclaimed and comprehensive study for the US Public Health Service, begun in the 1960s. Results have been published in the Journal of the American Medical Association, April 1995 (co-authored by Doctors Lee and Hsieh). The conclusion: as the amount of exercise increases, rates of death from all major causes are reduced. Those who exercise more can statistically predict that they will live longer than they would when sedentary or with minimal exertion. His extensive research has also shown that the more calories burned, the greater the benefit.

Starting exercise after the age of 60 can lengthen life. Dr. Kenneth Cooper, founder and director of the Cooper Clinic and the Cooper Institute of Aerobic Research, has volumes of research on various aspects of this topic. Findings also reveal that men of all ages who exercise regularly experience a 60% reduction in heart attacks, while women show a 40% reduction.

Breast cancer reduced in females who regularly exercised during the childbearing years. This was reported in the Journal of the National Cancer Institute.

Older runners reduced their risk of heart disease, as they increased weekly mileage. Research in the National Runners Health Study shows that as runners increase their weekly mileage, they experience a reduced ratio of total cholesterol to the "bad" LDL cholesterol. Higher mileage runners also tend to reduce systolic blood pressure, while cutting down on waist and hip fat. The reduction in LDL among those running 40+ miles per week represents a 29-30% reduction in heart attack risk.

Exercise reduced death rate in women. This was the conclusion by Lissner et al, in the American Journal of Epidemiology (Jan 1996), from an extensive study of Swedish women. The researchers also found that reducing physical activity increased risk of death.

Sherman et al found that the most active women exercisers cut their death rate by one third (American Heart Journal, Nov 1994).

Colon cancer and GI hemorrhage decreased by regular exercise. Several studies show a 30% reduction of colon cancer among regular exercisers. Gastrointestinal hemorrhage research is reported by Pahor et al (JAMA Aug 1994).

Better thinking: Spirduso (Physical Fitness, Aging, and Psychomotor Speed: a review in Journal of Gerontology 1980) found that those who regularly exercised performed better on tests of cognitive functioning.

Less depression, better attitude: Eysenck et al (Adv Behav Res Ther 1982) found that active folks were more likely to be better adjusted compared with sedentary individuals. Folkins et al (American Journal of Psychology 1981) showed that exercise improves self-confidence and self-esteem. Weyerer et al reported that patients who exercised and were given counseling did better than with counseling alone (Sports Medicine, Feb 1994). Blumenthal et al (Journal of Gerontology 1989) found that exercise training reduces depression in healthy older men, and Martinsen et al (British Medical Journal 1985) found exercise very effective in populations with major depression. Camancho et al (American Journal of Epidemiology 1991) found that newcomers to exercise were at no greater risk for depression than those who had exercised regularly.

Running and Joint Health

Running does not predispose joints to arthritis Dan Wnorowski, MD, has written a paper which reviews research on the effects of running and joint health. He believes that the majority of the relevant literature during the past decade on this topic finds little or no basis that running increases arthritis risk. Wnorowski goes on to say that a recent MRI study indicates that the prevalence of knee meniscus abnormalities in asymptomatic marathon runners is no different than sedentary controls.

- "Studies have shown that joint nourishment is entirely based upon keeping joints in motion"
  Charles Jung, MD from Group Health Cooperative website.
- "We don't see marathon runners having more joint injuries than sedentary folks. Simply put, active people have less joint injury." P.Z. Pearce, MD from Group Health Cooperative website.
- "Running offers up to 12 years of protection from onset of osteoarthritis." BBC website 16 Oct 2002.
- "Painless running or other activities which are aerobic and make you fit help keep you vigorous for longer." Professor Jim Fries, Stanford University (commenting upon results of his research at Stanford on aging exercisers).
- "Inactivity was once thought to prevent arthritis and protect fragile arthritic joints from further damage. More recent research has demonstrated the opposite." Benjamin Ebert, MD, Ph.D., as quoted in Dr. Larry Smith's website.
- "The notion that sports and recreational activities cause an inevitable wear on the joints just does not hold up when the scientific studies are evaluated. Few competitive or recreational long distance runners suffer severe joint injuries and many regular runners can recall how long and how often they have run." Ross Hauser, M.D, and Marion Hauser M.S.R.D. as quoted in Dr. Larry Smith's website.

Older runners reported pain and disability only 25% as often as those who didn't run. A study conducted by Fries, et al.

"Running or jogging does not increase the risk of osteoarthritis even though traditionally we thought it was a disease of wear and tear." Dr. Fries, from his study.

"Reasonably long-duration, high-mileage running need not be associated with premature degenerative joint disease of the lower extremities." Panush et al, "Is Running Associated with Degenerative Joint Disease?" JAMA 1986. Subjects were at least 50 years old, mean number of years running: 12, mean weekly mileage 28.

No increase in degenerative joint disease in runners. "Competitive sports increase joint risk—but running risk is low". Lane, et al, "Risk of Osteoarthritis (OA) With Running and Aging: Five Year Longitudinal Study". Studied runners 50-72 years old. Findings were similar to the conclusions of a study in 1989.

"Running seems to be devoid of adverse effects leading to knee degeneration, compared with other sports." Kujala et al, "Knee Osteoarthritis in Former Runners, Soccer Players, Weight Lifters, and Shooters" (Arthritis & Rheumatism, 1995).

"Runners averaging 66 years of age have not experienced accelerated development of radiographic OA (Osteoarthritis) of the knee compared with non-runner controls." Lane et al, Journal of Rheumatology 1998.

"Older individuals with OA of the knees (not end stage) benefit from exercise." Ettinger et al, JAMA 1997.

"Little or no risk of OA with lifelong distance running." Konradsen et al, (AJSM 1990) studied a group that tends to abuse the orthopedic limits (former competitive runners) that ran 20-40 km per week for 40 years. Other interesting studies include Lane et al, JAMA 1989, Kujala et al, Arthritis & Rheumatism 1995.

Note: The American Heart Association has a wonderful document that details the varied and significant benefits from exercise, citing 107 research sources. You can search for this on the internet under "AHA Medical/Scientific Statement".

How to Run Better as You Get Older

- Take control of your training by inserting rest before it is needed
- When doing a challenging workout, stay below the threshold of irritation of weak links
- Use walk breaks, earlier and more often as the years go on
- Replace shoes before they are worn out—alternate 2-3 shoes
- Avoid saturated fat and trans fat in your diet
- Eat small meals every 2-3 hours
- Use your training journal—plan ahead, record, adjust
- Insert rest and slow down—before you are forced to do so
- Keep muscles/tendons active and resilient by walking and massage (self massage most often)
- Have a running project every week—scenic or social run, race, trail, etc.
- Write your running book in your training journal
- When you're unsure about your running technique, run easier
- Be positive!

The key to running until you're 100 or so, is to maintain good health and nutrition, stay within your capabilities, and exercise regularly enough to maintain the adaptations you've worked so hard to achieve. By putting into action the age appropriate suggestions in this book, it's possible to enjoy running more while reducing aches and pains.

Every year I communicate with hundreds who put on their first running shoes past the age of 60. One of the fastest growing age groups in many parts of the running world is the 80+ division. I've met and heard of several runners in their 90s who still glow from each run—every other day or so. Running is one of the few recreational activities that can often be enjoyed into advanced ages. It is obvious to me that while we need to be more conservative as the years go by, we benefit from, and are penalized by, the same principles of training that apply to 20 year olds.

Maturity helps most runners to concentrate better and to organize their training. Those in their 30s and early 40s can often improve without focusing on specific workouts or balancing them with rest. At some point, however, fatigue and injury lead many to mistakenly assume that they are too old to run, or that their best running years are behind them.

I've been fortunate to hear from thousands of runners in their 50s (and sometimes in their 60s) who are not only in the best physical condition of their lives—they are running faster than they did when they were 30 or 40. If you want to improve performance, you'll find the guidelines in this book so you can take advantage of improved concentration, patience, and a better sense of balance—especially between stress and rest. While faster times give the ego a wonderful midlife boost, the most powerful running rewards follow even the slowest of runs...and the slowest of runners.

In many ways, running is more important to older runners. When other physical capabilities are reduced, runners can often run farther than they have ever run. While all of us tend to become more introspective as we age, runners spend positive time with themselves sorting through strengths, solving problems, and feeling great afterward. The wonderful attitude boost and vitality generated by a run connects runners of all ages: 9 years old......or 90.

This book is designed to give you control of your running, in this very important time of your life. You'll learn what elements need to be changed as the years go by, how much rest is ideal, when it should be inserted, pace adjustments, walk breaks, and much more. If you want to improve, you'll find proven ways to tell how much can be expected, and what you're capable of running at any point in time. The tools in this book allow you to be the captain of your running destiny and your attitude.

This book is written as one runner to another. It is the result of about 50 years of running, and having been the "coach" to more than 200,000 runners in one way or another for over 35 years. None of the advice inside is offered as medical advice. To get help in this area, see a doctor or appropriate medical expert.

Major Differences as You Get Older

As mentioned above, research shows that runners don't experience any more joint problems as they age than those who don't run regularly. But I have known runners who've ignored common sense, pushed through repeated warning signs, and encountered self-imposed permanent damage. It is clear to me that if you walk and run regularly, below the threshold of irritation, your orthopedic components continue to adapt and maintain their functions better, over a longer period of time.

Mature runners often compare themselves to old cars. Due to continued wear and tear, there are a series of aches and pains that will be experienced. If you make the right conservative training adaptations, most runners can reduce the flare-ups, and keep going when the "weak links" complain. In dealing with the problems, you get to know yourself better, and can prevent problems. Most of the adjustments involve adding strategic rest, such as running fewer days per week, taking more walk breaks, and inserting extra recovery time when aches and pains increase.

Competitive runners must ask themselves a difficult question, every year or two: How much risk do I want to take by running faster? Those who continue to push the limits usually reduce the number of years that they can enjoy running. This is where real maturity counts. Make a choice and take the consequences. It is my recommendation that running enjoyment be the primary goal—if you want to be moving down the road when the clock strikes 100.

If you're not afraid to continue learning and adjusting, there's no reason why you can't enjoy the running experience for decades to come. The personal running achievement which gives me the most pride is my injury-free period of about 30 years—because I made the conservative adjustments you'll find in this book.

How to deal with the recovery rate slowdown

After the age of 30, it takes longer for the legs to feel fresh and bouncy after a strenuous run. Most runners don't notice this (or don't want to admit it) until they reach the age of 40. By adding conservative training ingredients, injury risk drops dramatically. Many veterans find that they run faster while covering fewer miles per week, especially when running fewer days per week.

The best way I've found to speed recovery is to include enough days off from running. This allows the body to rebuild and adapt to efficient running. In general, it is better to run more miles on your running days and run fewer days per week. The following table has recommendations for the number of days one can run, based upon age, when runners:

- Are experiencing more injuries, aches and pains, or orthopedic problems;
- Are not recovering quickly between runs or races;
- Are experiencing a slowdown in race times.

(If you're not having any of these problems you can run the number of days per week that you wish)

Recommended number of running/walking days per week by age:

(You can walk or cross train on 2-3 other days if desired)

35 and under: no more than 5 days a week
36-45: no more than 4 running days a week
46-59: run every other day
60 + : 3 days a week
70 + : 2 running days and 1 long walk day
80 + : One longer run, one shorter run, and one long walk

Note: the day before the long run should be a day of rest

More walk breaks

The simple addition of more walk breaks, from the beginning of the run, has allowed many mature runners to maintain mileage while reducing aches and pains. By warming up the legs more gently, through walk breaks, many runners feel better on every run, reduce injuries, and improve the quality of the latter part of the run.

I've adjusted the walk breaks for age and pace as follows. For more information, read the Run-Walk-Run™ section of this book.

Pace per mile	Run Amount	Walk Amount
7:00	4 minutes	20 seconds
7:30	4 minutes	20 seconds
8:00	4 minutes	30 seconds
8:30	3 minutes	30 seconds

9:00	2 minutes	30 seconds
9:30	2 minutes	40 seconds
10:00-11:29	1.5 minutes	30 seconds
11:30-13:29	1 minute	30 seconds
13:30-14:59	1 minute	1 minute (or run 30 seconds and walk 30 seconds)
15:00-16:59	30 seconds	45 seconds (or run 1 min and walk 1:30)
17:00-20:00	20-30 seconds	1 minute

A longer and easier warm-up

As the years go by, it takes longer (during an individual run) for the legs to feel good. Here is what I recommend:

- At least 5 minutes of gentle walking,
- Then, 5 minutes of walking at varied paces. Even if you walk a bit faster during the second 5 minutes, use a short stride.
- Insert some run breaks into your walk for 10 minutes. Start with 10-20 seconds of running followed by a minute of walking, and then gradually shift to 1 minute of running and 1 minute of walking.
- Then, ease into your running pace and the run-walk-run frequency for that day.
- It is always better to be conservative.

Note: If you are doing a speed workout, after the warm-up above, add 4 each of the Acceleration-Gliders and Cadence Drills, described later in this book.

Breaking up your daily mileage into 2 or 3 sessions

A runner recently told me that his running really took off when he retired. He was running more miles per day, without injury, by running 2 or 3 shorter runs. These were strategically placed throughout the day so that they energized him for at least an hour afterward, and reminded him of "recess breaks" during elementary school.

Fast running takes more out the legs

Runners in their 40s and 50s can sometimes do the same workouts they ran in their 20s and 30s—but they will pay dearly for this. Running at your limits, after a certain age, can produce negative consequences. While it is true that speed training and racing significantly increase the chance of injury, there are safer ways to train to improve times at any age. It's a fact that as you age, recovery elements must be added to the program. I don't recommend speed reps after 80 years of age, but there is some speed benefit from my Cadence Drills and Acceleration Gliders, mentioned in this book.

Note: Be sure to get your doctor's clearance before attempting a speed program

Rest intervals between speed repetitions:
(400m means 400 meters, or one lap around a track or .25 mile)

	40-50	51-60	61-65	66-70	71-75	76-80
400 meter:	200m walk	300m walk	350m walk	400m walk	500m walk	600m walk
800 meter:	300m walk	350m walk	400m walk	500m walk	600m walk	700m walk
1 mile:	400m walk	450m walk	500m walk	600m walk	700m walk	800m walk

Plan for motivation

There are many suggestions in this book for enhancing motivation to run. Just having a plan will bestow a sense of confidence that is lacking in those who just get out there. Thousands of over 40-year-old runners, who lost motivation without a plan, lit the fire again by setting up a goal schedule. Even after sickness or other interruptions, the framework of your plan can provide direction. It's motivating to become part of the process of improvement.

Planning pays off

When you have a schedule, each run has a purpose: stress relief, endurance, form improvement, etc. As in the completion of a puzzle, the completion of the daily workout is one more piece locked into the overall vision of your running life. The early workouts stimulate the muscles to make gentle adaptations which prepare the body to work harder weeks or months later. The non running days are more important for mature runners, compared with the hard workouts. There must be adequate rest to allow the muscles, etc., to rebuild and improve internal engineering. As you look over your plan for the next few months, you'll realize that you are moving forward, while connected with your running past, heading for the future. You're more likely to achieve your potential if you use a plan—even if you have no performance goals at all.

Controlling injuries and fatigue by inserting enough rest

Staying injury-free is the primary reason runners, especially mature runners, improve. By balancing stress with rest, you can control the gradual increases—and prevent injury. It is crucial to be conservative. By making adjustments at the first signs of possible injury, you'll avoid a much greater period of downtime later. At the first sign of a possible injury, take at least 3 days off and treat the injured area. If you're experiencing more fatigue, increase the walk breaks, decrease distance, and don't run more often than 3 days a week.

Fine-tuning from previous years

As much as we would like to improve memory, this will probably not happen. Making good notes in your journal will allow you to analyze the causes of aches and pains, and training problems. Even if you can't run faster at 90, you can run smarter, and prevent problems. Use the margins of your journal. Tell yourself what you want to do the next time to avoid problems. You'll help yourself greatly by tracking the adjustments. As you embark on another goal in future years, you'll have a better blueprint, because you've improved the original plan through adjustments to your reality.

I believe that a great deal of the satisfaction we receive emerges from what we do on a regular basis. I've seen many people improve their outlook on life itself when they use a proven plan to improve their running. Following and adjusting the plan to running success is almost always a life-changing experience, for the better.

Blood sugar issues

Many runners develop blood sugar problems as they age. Read the chapter in this book on blood sugar maintenance.

Health issues

Running makes you feel better as it enhances health potential and life expectancy. Many runners have told me that their running gave them the only signs of serious health risks—which led to early detection and successful treatment. Find a doctor who supports running and wants to work with you to sustain the highest level of wellness.

Goals and Priorities

Most of the runners I've coached, over the age of 40, have noticed an improvement in their ability to focus and prioritize, compared with a decade or two earlier in life. Maturity usually bestows the confidence to become captain of your running ship. This can be a double-edged sword. If you get too "driven", your improved concentration powers can push you into fatigue and injury. The following are only some of the ways you can steer this ship. Take out a pencil as you read through this chapter, and assign a priority to each component, then jot down other goals that you would like to realize. Revisit these priorities each week to ensure that you stay

Running enjoyment

Find a way to enjoy parts of every run—even the faster training. Most of your runs should be....mostly enjoyable. You increase the pleasure by ensuring that there are social or scenic runs every week. Too often, busy people leave these out. Take control of your enjoyment of running and life by scheduling the fun sessions first.

Health issues

In the next section are some health tips particularly helpful to older runners. It's important to monitor your risk of heart disease— particularly if you have a family history of this or have experienced the appropriate risk factors. Runners die from cardiovascular causes every year, who could have avoided this by getting the right tests and taking action. Usually, runners with heart conditions can continue to run while managing their problem. For any questions in this area, see a doctor who supports running and exercise as long as possible.

Stay injury free

The single reason why runners improve and enjoy running is that they don't get injured. Make a list of past injuries, and new aches that have been experienced lately. After reading the injury section of this book, make the needed adjustments. As you eliminate the stress, and insert strategic rest, you can eliminate most of your injuries.

Note: There's more injury information in *Galloway's Book on Running*, 2nd Edition.

Avoiding overuse or burnout

With each decade, we must become more sensitive to the early warning signs of over-training. Unfortunately, we often ignore these or don't know what they are. Your training journal is a wonderful tool for noting any possible ache, pain, loss of desire, unusual fatigue that lingers, etc. If you develop an injury, you can review your journal and often find the reasons. This helps you to become more vigilant to possible problems and make conservative adjustments in your training plan to reduce injury risk.

Time goals

I talk to many runners every year that set lifetime personal records in races in their 40s and 50s. But everyone will experience a time when it becomes very difficult to improve, and a growing number of aches and pains when attempting to maximize potential. Training programs for various distances are noted in *Galloway's Book on Running*, 2nd Edition, *Marathon*, *A Year-Round Plan*, *Testing Yourself*, & *Half Marathon*. In this book you'll find guidelines which will help you adjust the training for your age.

What is a realistic goal for you?

The next few chapters will help you answer this question. You'll be introduced to a test that can tell you your current running potential in several events. Then, you'll learn how to choose the amount of improvement you want to shoot for. But remember, time goals should be placed far behind your first two priorities: enjoying each run & staying injury free.

Health Alert!!

Medical check

Check with your doctor's office before you start a strenuous training program. Keep the doctor informed of any irregularities in your cardiovascular system or aches and pains that could be signs of health risks or injuries. At first, just tell the doctor or head nurse how much running you plan to be doing over the next year. Almost every person will be given the green light to continue running as you move into the mature decades of life. If your doctor recommends against your running plans, ask why. Since there are so few people who cannot train even for strenuous goals if they use a liberal run-walk-run ™ formula, I suggest that you get a second opinion if your doctor tells you not to run. The best medical advisor is one who wants you to get the type of physical activity that engages you—unless there are significant reasons not to do so.

Note: the information in this book is offered as advice from one runner to another, and not meant to be medical advice. Having a doctor/advisor will help you through some problems more quickly. A responsive and supportive medical "coach" will improve confidence and motivation, while reducing anxiety.

Heart disease and running

Running tends to have a beneficial effect on cardiovascular disease. But more runners die of heart disease than any other cause, and are susceptible to the same risk factors as sedentary people. Like most other citizens, runners at risk usually don't know that they are at risk. I know of a number of runners who have suffered heart attacks and strokes who probably could have prevented them if they had taken a few simple tests. Some of these are listed below, but check with your doctor if you have any questions or concerns.

This short section is offered as a guide to help you take charge of your cardiovascular health. Running and walking bestow a high level of healthy conditioning of the most important organ, help to increase longevity, while improving quality of life. As always, you need to get advice about your individual situation from a doctor who knows you.

Risk factors—get checked if you have two of these—or one that is serious

- Family history
- Poor lifestyle habits earlier in life
- High fat/high cholesterol diet
- Have smoked or still smoke
- Obese or severely overweight
- High blood pressure (Good to be under 135/85, Best if under 125/75)
- High cholesterol (Good to be under 180, Best if under 150)
- High blood sugar (Good to be under 100)

Tests can tell you if you are at risk

- Stress Test—heart is monitored during a run that gradually increases in difficulty. This test will screen out some at risk, but many with real problems fall through the cracks.
- Cholesterol Screening—a number that is below 180 is good and 150 is excellent. Ask your doctor about your individual situation and the variation between your HDL particles (better to have a higher percentage) and your LDL (particles that can cause problems).
- C reactive Protein—has been an indicator of increased risk
- Heart scan—an electronic scan of the heart which shows calcification, and possible narrowing of arteries. A higher than normal reading does not mean blockage but may indicate the need for more tests.
- Radioactive dye test—very effective in locating specific blockages. Talk to your doctor about this.
- Carotid ultrasound test—helps to tell if you're at risk for stroke
- Ankle-brachial test—denotes plaque buildup in arteries throughout the body

None of these are foolproof. But by working with your cardiologist, you can increase your chance of living until the muscles just won't propel you further down the road—past the age of 100.

Choosing a doctor

A growing number of family practice physicians are advocates for fitness. If your doctor is not very supportive, ask the nurses in the office if there is one in the same office group or elsewhere, who might be. The doctors who are physical fitness advocates are very often more positive and energetic, and maintain information about the latest research about how exercise reduces disease and prolongs the quality of life.

The running grapevine may help you find a supportive doctor

Ask the staff at local running stores, running club members, or long-term runners. They will usually know of several doctors in your town who runners visit with various medical problems. Doctors tell me that compared with their other patients, runners tend to ask more questions, and want to prevent disease. Runners tend to maintain a high level of activity until the very end of life. You want a doctor who will welcome this, and serve as your "health coach." Choose someone who will work with you to avoid injury, sickness, and other health setbacks.

Should I run when I have a cold?

There are so many individual health issues associated with a cold that you must talk with a doctor before you exercise when you have an infection.

Lung infection—don't run! A virus in the lungs can move into the heart and kill you. Lung infections are usually indicated by coughing.

Common cold? There are many infections that initially indicate a normal cold but are not—they may be much more serious. At least call your doctor's office to get clearance before running. Be sure to explain how much you are running, and what, if any medication you are taking.

Infections of the throat and above the neck—most runners will be given the OK, but check with the doctor.

Risk of speed

There is an increased risk of both injuries and cardiovascular events during speed sessions. Be sure to get your doctor's OK before beginning a speed program. Don't ever continue to run—even 10 yards—when you suspect that you may have an injury or a real cardiovascular problem. Stop, take an extra 2-3 days off and get medical advice if necessary. The advice inside this book is generally conservative, but when in doubt, take more rest, more days off, and run slower. In other words...be more conservative.

Walk breaks let you erase fatigue and damage to the legs and body"

The Galloway Run-Walk-Run™ Method

Walk breaks....

- Give you control over the way you feel at the end
- Allow older runners and heavier runners to cover any distance they wish, and recover fast
- Erase fatigue
- Push back your fatigue wall
- Allow for endorphins to collect during each walk break—you feel good!
- Break up the distance into manageable units ("two more minutes")
- Speed recovery
- Reduce the chance of aches, pains and injury
- Allow you to feel good afterward—performing daily activities you need to do after the run
- Give you all of the endurance of the distance of each session—without the pain

Walk breaks have allowed runners in their 40s to run faster than they did in their 30s, and those over 50 to maintain a higher level of running consistency. Over 60 runners who follow the guidelines noted below have told me that they experience fewer aches and pains than in their 30s or 40s. I doubt that you will find any training component that will help you in more ways than my run-walk-run ™ method. I continue to be amazed, every week, as I receive the success stories of older runners because they took charge of their run by inserting walk breaks from the beginning. Many improve their finish times when they find the right ratio. When placed appropriately for the individual, fatigue is erased, motivation improves, running enjoyment is enhanced, and the runner feels confident and finishes with strength.

Walk before you get tired

Most of us, even when untrained, can walk for several miles before fatigue sets in, because walking is an activity that we are bio-engineered to do for hours. Running is harder because you must lift your body off the ground and then absorb the shock of the landing, over and over. It's a well-known scientific fact that continuous use of the running muscles leads to increased fatigue, and more injuries. But if you walk before your running muscles start to get tired, you allow the muscle to recover instantly—increasing your capacity for exercise while reducing the chance of next-day soreness, and long-term injury.

The "method" part involves having a strategy. By using a ratio of running and walking, you'll manage your fatigue. Using this fatigue-reduction tool early gives you the muscle resources and the mental confidence to cope with any challenges that can come later. Even when you don't need the extra strength and resiliency bestowed by the method, you will feel better during and after your run, and finish knowing that you could have gone farther.

"The run-walk method is very simple: you run for a short segment and then take a walk break, and keep repeating this pattern."

Walk breaks allow you to take control over fatigue, in advance, so that you can enjoy every run. By taking them early and often, you can feel strong even after a run that is very long for you. Beginners will alternate very short run segments with short walks. Even elite runners find that walk breaks on long runs allow them to recover faster. There is no need to be totally exhausted at the end of a run— even a 30 miler.

A short and gentle walking stride
It's better to walk slowly, with a short stride. There has been some irritation of the shins, when runners or walkers maintain a stride that is too long. Relax and enjoy the walk.

No need to ever eliminate the walk breaks
Some runners assume that they must work toward the day when they don't have to take any walk breaks at all. This is up to the individual, but is not recommended. Remember that you decide

what ratio of run-walk-run to use. There is no rule that requires you to hold to any ratio on a given day. As you adjust the run-walk according to how you feel, you gain control over your fatigue.

I've run for about 50 years, and I enjoy running more than ever because of walk breaks. During and after almost every run, I am energized and mentally alert. I would not be able to run almost every day if I didn't insert the walk breaks early and often. I start most runs taking a short walk break every minute. By 2 miles I am usually walking every 3-4 minutes. By 5 miles the ratio often goes to every 7-10 minutes. But there are days every year when I stay at 3 minutes and even a few days at 1 minute.

The run-walk-run™ ratio that you use will vary from day to day. The more conservative you are, the more enjoyment you can expect from your running—day after day.

How to keep track of the walk breaks

There are several watches which can be set to beep when it's time to walk, and then beep again when it's time to start up again. Check our website (www.jeffgalloway.com) or a good running store for advice in this area.

Run-Walk-Run™ Ratios

After having coached over 100,000 runners using walk breaks, I've come up with the following suggested ratios for runners over about 45 years old:

Pace per mile	Run Amount -	Walk Amount
7:00	4 minutes	20 seconds
7:30	4 minutes	20 seconds
8:00	4 minutes	30 seconds
8:30	3 minutes	30 seconds
9:00	2 minutes	30 seconds
9:30	2 minutes	40 seconds
10:00-11:29	1.5 minutes	30 seconds
11:30-13:29	1 minute	30 seconds
13:30-14:59	1 minute	1 minute (or run 30 seconds and walk 30 seconds)
15:00-16:59	30 seconds	45 seconds (or run 1 min and walk 1:30)
17:00-20:00	20-30 seconds	1 minute

In general, I've found that older runners benefit more from shorter running segments, with more frequent walk breaks, even when the walks are shorter.

Note: you may always divide each of the amounts by 2. Example: instead of running 4 minutes/walking 30 seconds, you could run 2 minutes and walk 15 seconds. This allows for you to walk through a water stop, if you've just walked at a mile marker.

What Pace Is Today?

Mature runners suffer greatly when they run too fast, especially on long runs. But what is the correct pace? In this chapter we'll answer this question. Even if you're not interested in running faster, my prediction formulas listed below will tell you the right pace for you. For each day, you can determine which goals are realistic for you, how much improvement may be possible, and whether you are on track for the goal at certain check points. At the end of the program these scheduled time trials will tell you the performance you can expect on a good day, and how to make adjustments for temperature.

Regular testing takes the guesswork out of goal setting. You may have to rein in your ego, because it will often try to talk you into goals that are not within your current capabilities. The "magic miles" allow you to adjust your workouts based upon the reality of your current performance potential. You can then avoid the disappointment of pursuing unrealistic goals.

Right for Me....

Note: My book *A Year-Round Plan* has 52 weeks of workouts to help you train for as many as 4 significant race distances in a year.

Guidelines for using the formulas:

- You have done the training necessary for the goal—according to the training programs in *Galloway's Book on Running,* 2ND Edition, *A Year-Round Plan, Half Marathon, Marathon* or *Testing Yourself.*
- You are not injured.
- You run with an even-paced effort, taking walk breaks as needed.
- The weather on goal race day is not adverse. Weather conditions that would slow you down include temperatures above 60F, strong headwinds, heavy rain or snow, etc.

The "Magic Mile"

This one mile time trial (TT) has become my favorite evaluation tool, because it is easy to do and has predicted performances very accurately. The experience gained from coaching over 200,000 runners (over more than 30 years), has helped me develop the following formulas. Here's how!

1. Go to a track, or other accurately measured course.

2. Warm up by walking for 5 minutes, then running 1 minute and walking 1 minute, then jogging an easy 800 meter (half mile or two laps around a track).

3. Do 4 acceleration-gliders. These are listed in the "Drills" chapter.

4. Walk for 3-4 minutes.

5. Run the one mile TT—a hard effort for 4 laps—following the walk-break suggestions in this chapter. Start your watch at the beginning and keep it running until the end of the 4th lap.

6. On your first race, don't run all-out from the start—ease into your pace after the first half (2 laps).

7. Warm down by reversing the warm-up.

8. A school track is the best venue. Don't use a treadmill because they tend to be notoriously un-calibrated, and often tell you that you ran farther or faster than you really did.

9. On each successive TT, adjust pace in order to run a faster time than you did on the previous one.

10. Use the formula below to see what time is predicted in the goal races

"How hard should I run the test?"

Never run all out. In your first "magic mile" (MM) you'll run just a little faster than you have been running. On each successive MM, your mission is to beat the previous time. After about 4-6 of these, most runners are running close to their potential time for this distance.

At this point you will run the first lap slightly slower than you think you can average. Take a short walk break as noted in the walk break suggestions in this chapter. If you aren't huffing and puffing, you can pick up the pace a bit on the second lap. If you are huffing after the first lap, then just hold your pace on lap two. Most runners benefit from taking a walk break after the second lap. At the end of lap 3, the walk break is optional. It is OK to be breathing hard on the last lap. If you are slowing down on the last lap, start a little slower on the next test. At the end of the program, when you finish, you should feel like you couldn't run more than about half a lap farther at that pace (if that). You may find that you don't need many walk breaks during the test—experiment and adjust. As always, tell your doctor that you want to run a fast one mile run, (not sprinting) after building up to this effort over several weeks.

GALLOWAY'S PREDICTION FORMULAS

To predict your per mile pace in longer distances from the one mile TT: (4 laps around the track)

5K: Take your one mile time and add 33 seconds
10K: Take your one mile time and multiply by 1.15
Half Marathon: Take your one mile time and multiply by 1.2
Marathon: Take your one mile time and multiply by 1.3
Long run pace: 2-3 minutes per mile slower than Marathon predicted pace

Example:

Mile time: 10:00 (or 10.0 minutes)
For 5K time, add 33 seconds: 10:33 is predicted mile pace for a 5K (31:33 for a 5K)
For 10K time, multiply 10 x 1.15 = 11.5 min/mi (11:30) x 6.2 (mi in a 10K)
For half marathon time multiply 10.0 x 1.2 = 12 min/mi (12:00 x 13.1 mi)
For marathon time, multiply 10 x 1.3 = 13 min/mi (13:00 x 26.2 mi)
Long run pace should be 15-15:30 per mile

One Mile Time	(add 33 sec) 5K Pace	(x 1.15) 10K Pace	(x 1.2) Half Mar	(x 1.3) Marathon
5:00	5:33	5:45	6:00	6:30
5:30	6:03	6:19	6:37	7:09
6:00	6:33	6:54	7:12	7:48
6:30	7:03	7:25	7:48	8:28
7:00	7:33	8:03	8:24	9:06
7:30	8:03	8:37	9:00	9:45
8:00	8:33	9:12	9:36	10:24
8:30	9:03	9:46	10:12	11:03
9:00	9:33	10:21	11:48	11:42
9:30	10:03	10:57	11:24	12:21
10:00	10:33	11:30	12:00	13:00

10:30	11:03	12:04	12:36	13:39
11:00	11:33	12:39	13:12	14:18
11:30	12:03	13:19	13:48	14:57
12:00	12:33	13:48	14:24	15:36
12:30	13:03	14:22	15:00	16:15
13:00	13:33	14:57	15:36	16:54
13:30	14:03	15:31	16:12	17:33
14:00	14:33	16:06	16:48	18:12
14:30	15:03	16:38	17:24	18:51
15:00	15:33	17:15	18:00	19:30
15:30	16:03	17:49	18:36	20:09
16:00	16:33	18:24	19:12	20:48

Walk breaks during the one mile test

Pace of the race/per mi	# of seconds walking
8:00	5-10 sec every 2 laps
8:30	8-12 sec every 2 laps
9:00	10-15 sec every 2 laps
9:30	12-18 sec every 2 laps
10:00	5-8 sec every lap
10:30	7-10 sec every lap
11:00	9-12 sec every lap
11:30	10-15 sec every lap
12:00	11-16 sec every lap
12:30	12-17 sec every lap
13:00	13-18 sec every lap
13:30	14-19 sec every lap
14:00	15-20 sec every lap
14:30	16-21 sec every lap
15:00	17-22 sec every lap
15:30	18-23 sec every lap
16:00	19-24 sec every lap

The "leap of faith" goal prediction

It is OK to choose a time for your goal race which is faster than is predicted by your pre-test. Since you are starting 3-6 months ahead of the goal race, you can expect to improve by doing the speed training, the long runs and the drills. For prediction purposes, as you take this "leap" to a goal, I suggest no more than a 3% improvement in a 3-6 month training program.

> **Note:** In your first race at any distance, run easily "to finish". After completing one race you can work toward a faster time—if you wish.

1. Run the one mile time trial.
2. Use the formulas above to predict what you could run now, if you were trained for the goal distance.
3. Choose the amount of improvement during program (1-3%).
4. Subtract this from # 2—this is your goal time.

How much can be your "leap of faith"?

Pre-test prediction in the 5K	3% Improvement (Over a 3-6 month training program)
40 minutes	1 minute 12 seconds
33 minutes	60 seconds
28 minutes	50 seconds
25 minutes	45 seconds
20 minutes	36 seconds
17 minutes	31 seconds

Pre-test prediction in the half marathon	
3:00	2:54:36
2:30	2:25:30
2:00	1:56:24

Pre-test prediction in the marathon	
6:30	6:18:18
6:00	5:49:12
5:30	5:20:06
5:00	4:51:00
4:30	4:21:54
4:00	3:52:48

The key to goal setting is keeping your ego in check. From my experience, I have found that a 3% improvement is realistic, but challenging. This means that if your 5K time is predicted to be 30 minutes, then it is realistic to assume that you could lower it by 54 seconds if you do the speed training and the long runs as noted on my training schedules, during the training plan.

In all of these situations, however, everything must come together to produce the predicted result. Even runners who shoot for a 3% improvement and do all the training as described, achieve their goal slightly more than 50% of the time during a racing season. There are many factors that determine a time goal in a marathon that are outside of your control: weather, terrain, infection, etc.

Note: You'll find training plans for 1mi through 5K distances in my book, Testing Yourself. Training schedules for 5K through marathon can be found in *A Year-Round Plan*. Half marathon, 5K and 10K schedules are available in *Galloway's Book on Running*, 2nd Edition. Marathon training is scheduled in *Marathon*. My new *Half-Marathon* book has the training necessary for that popular distance.

Final reality check

Take the last 3 TT, and eliminate the slowest time. Average the 2 remaining times to get a good prediction in your goal race. *If the tests are predicting a time that is slower than the goal you've been training for, adjust your race goal accordingly.* It is strongly recommended that you run the first one-third of your goal race a few seconds a mile slower than the pace predicted by the test average. As always, adjust race day goal for the temperature.

Use a journal!

Read the chapter on using a journal. Your chance of reaching your goal increases greatly when you use this very important instrument. Psychologically, you start taking responsibility for the fulfillment of your mission when you use a journal. *Jeff Galloway's Training Journal* has one year's worth of journal entries, with help in setting up your training and journal.

Prediction strategies

During my competitive years, and the first decade that I worked with other runners, I found a very beneficial prediction tool in Computerized Running Training Programs by Gerry Purdy and James Gardner. This book has been revised and re-published in print and software as Running Trax, by Track and Field News. This is a great resource that I highly recommend.

Mature Runner's Checklist

Running is one of the few experiences in life where you can feel somewhat free of most of the demands and expectations that usually burden us. One of the liberating feelings you get from running comes from its simplicity—the minimal require- ments. You can run from your home or office in most cases, using public streets or pedestrian walkways. Overall, I've found no experience in life that is as energizing that provides a wonderful attitude boost. I suggest making the necessary changes to your daily run to maximize these benefits.

Below are some items that can enhance the running experience. As you will see, the "top of the line" is not necessarily the best running item for you. For example, ordinary clothing and moderately priced shoes work well most of the time. You don't need to join a country club or invest in expensive exercise equipment. While running with another person can be motivating, you don't have to have a partner, and many mature runners run alone on most of their runs. It helps, however, to have a "support team" as you go through the training (running companions, doctors, running shoe experts), but you will probably meet these folks through the running "grapevine."

Shoes— the primary investment: "The best advice...is to get the best advice"

As we get older, we tend to experience a growing number of foot "issues." Most over 40 runners wisely decide to spend a little time on the choice of a good running shoe. After all, shoes are the only real equipment needed—and running store folks can deal with the "foot issues" in many cases. The shoe that is a good match for your feet can make running easier, by reducing blisters, foot fatigue and injuries.

Because there are so many different brands and models, shoe shopping can be confusing. Going to a good running store, staffed by helpful and knowledgeable runners, can cut the time required and can usually lead you to a better shoe choice than you would find by yourself. For more information on this see *Galloway's Book on Running*, 2ND Edition.

Bring your most worn shoes to the store with the most experienced staff

Even if your most worn shoes are your street shoes, show the wear pattern on the bottom to the staff person. Take along a pair of running shoes that has worked well for you also. As soon as you know a shoe will work for you, get a second pair and run in them for a short distance 1-2 days a week. This will gradually break in the new shoes and allow you to tell when the old shoes don't support you any more. Be sure to stop using the old ones before they are totally worn out.

Do I need a racing shoe?

In most cases, racing shoes only speed you up by a few seconds a mile—but this may be what you need to reach your goal. After several weeks, if you feel that your training shoes are too heavy or "clunky," look at some racing shoes. Caution: Mature runners usually find that a light weight training shoe is a better choice than a racing shoe. The minimal cushion in the latter will often compress during a race, producing a great deal of foot stress during the last few miles and afterward.

A watch

There are a lot of good, inexpensive watches which will give you accurate times on your workouts and races. Any watch that has a stopwatch function will do the job. Be sure to ask the staff person in the store how to use the stopwatch. A few watches can make walk breaks easier by "beeping" after each running segment and then again after the walking segment. For more information on current watches that do this, go to www.RunInjuryFree.com.

Clothing: comfort above all

The "clothing thermometer" at the end of this book can help you choose the appropriate apparel, based on current weather. In summer, you want to wear garments that are light and cool. On cold days, layering is the best strategy. As you experience difficulty with a variety of weather conditions, you'll find that some of the new technical fabrics can add comfort to the run—even on bad weather days. It is also OK to give yourself a fashionable outfit as a "reward" for running towards a certain goal.

A training journal

The journal is such an important component in running that I have written a chapter about it. By using a journal to plan ahead and then to later review mistakes, you take a major degree of control over your running future. You'll find it reinforcing to write down what you did each day, and miss that reinforcement when you skip. Once into the journal process, mature runners find that this is very satisfying.

Where to run

It helps to have several different venues. Try to find 2 or more options for each.

Long runs—scenic, interesting areas are best—with some pavement and some softer surface if possible. If you have a goal race that is run on pavement (most), it's best to run at least the last half of long runs on that type of surface.

Pace work—a track or any accurately-measured segment on roads or trails

Races—look carefully at the course—avoid hills, too many turns, or even too much flat terrain (if you usually train on rolling hills). Yes, in a non-hilly race, those who train on varied terrain will fatigue the flat running muscles more quickly.

Magic Mile time trials (TT)—a track is best. Most tracks are 400 meters (about a quarter mile).

Drills—any safe running area with a secure surface

Indoor—for the "bad weather days," it helps to have a treadmill or other venue available inside

Safety—top priority!

Pick a course that is away from car traffic, and is in a safe area—where crime is unlikely. Try to have 2 or more options for each of the components because variety can be very motivating.

Convenience

If you have several options near home and office, for each of the training components listed above, you will be more likely to do the workouts on your schedule—when you need to do them.

Surface

With the correct amount of cushion, and the selection of the right shoes for you, pavement should not produce extra shock to the legs or body. A smooth dirt or gravel path is a preferred surface for the easy days. But beware of an uneven surface, especially if you have weak ankles or foot problems. For your time trials, speed work and drills, you may have to talk to shoe experts to avoid blisters, etc. when running on certain types of surfaces. Avoid a road, trail, track or sidewalk with a slant—flat is best.

Picking a running companion

On long runs and on easy days, don't run with someone who is faster than you—unless that person is fully comfortable slowing down to an easy pace—that is…slow for you. Many mature runners get injured every year because they try to keep up with younger or faster friends—particularly on days when they should be running slowly. It is motivating to run with someone who will go slowly enough so that you can have a pleasant conversation. Share stories, jokes, problems if you wish, and you'll bond together in a very positive way. The friendships forged on runs can be the strongest and longest lasting—if you're not huffing and puffing (or puking) from trying to run at a pace that is too fast. On speed days, however, it sometimes helps to run with a person that is slightly faster than you, as long as you run each speed segment at the correct pace—for you.

Rewards

Rewards are important at all times. Be sensitive and reinforce your positive behaviors with items that will keep you motivated, and make the running experience a better one (more comfortable shoes, clothes, etc.).

Positive reinforcement works! Treating yourself to a smoothie after a hard run, taking a cool dip in a pool, going out to a special restaurant after a longer run—all of these can reinforce the successful completion of another week or month. Of particular benefit is having a snack, within 30 minutes after the completion of a run, which has about 200-300 calories, containing 80% carbohydrate and 20% protein. The products Accelerade and Endurox R4 are already formulated with this ratio for your convenience, and also give you a recovery boost.

An appointment on the calendar

Most mature runners run more days per year, when they schedule (in advance) their running days on a calendar or appointment book, staying 2 weeks ahead. You can schedule around other life activities, and lock the runs into your routine. Pretend that this is an appointment with your boss, or your most important client. Actually, you are your most important client!

Motivation to get out the door

There are 2 times when most runners feel challenged to run: early in the morning and at the end of the day. In the motivation section of this book, there are rehearsals for each of these situations. You will find it much easier to be motivated once you experience a regular series of runs that make you feel good. Yes, when you run and walk at the right pace, with the right preparation, you feel better, can relate to others better, and have more energy to enjoy the rest of the day.

Treadmills are just as good as streets for short runs

More and more runners are using treadmills for at least half of their runs—particularly those who have to watch small grandchildren. It's a fact that treadmills tend to register a distance and speed that is more than you've really done (usually they're not off by more than 10%). But if you run on a treadmill for the number of minutes assigned, at the effort level you are used to (no huffing and puffing), you will get close enough to the training effect you wish. To ensure that you have run enough miles, feel free to add 10% to your assigned mileage on the treadmill days.

Usually no need to eat before the run

Most runners don't need to eat before runs that are less than 6 miles. Among the exceptions are those with diabetes or severe blood sugar problems. Many runners feel better during a run when they have enjoyed a cup of coffee about an hour before the start. Caffeine engages the central nervous system, which gets all of the systems needed for exercise up and running to capacity, very quickly. When pressed, there are coffee extracts that can speed up the process, such as www.javette.com.

If your blood sugar is low, which often occurs in the afternoon, it helps to have a snack of 100-200 calories, which is composed of 80% carbohydrate and 20% protein. Have your snack about 30 minutes before the run. The Accelerade product has been very successful. Since turning 50, an energy bar and a cup of coffee have pushed me out the door on many occasions.

Physiological Improvements Occur at Any Age

Your body is a marvelous mechanism. Thousands of components inside are programmed to improve as you regularly run. This chapter provides a peek inside the muscle. But you'll also see how training can weave diverse elements together to help you move forward as a unit, improving health and fitness. The whole process is like a symphony of components, blending mind and body, heart and legs, left brain and right into an integrated team.

Our bodies are designed to improve through a series of challenges

I believe that distance running engages various systems in our bodies that connect us directly to our roots. Primitive man had to walk and run for survival—thousands of miles a year. Through millions of years of evolution, the muscles, tendons, bones, energy systems and cardiovascular components adapted and expanded the capacity of the human body to cover long distances. Over this extended period, a series of psychological rewards also developed. This is why we feel good when we run and walk at the correct (conservative) pace for us.

The "team" of heart, lungs, nerves, brain, etc.

Very often, in college and professional sports, a group of very talented individuals is defeated by a solid team of players with lesser ability. Running helps to mold your key body organs into a coordinated unit, i.e. to build such a solid team. When running within one's capacity, the right brain uses its intuitive and creative powers to solve problems, manage resources, and help us find the pace and amount of training that we can handle. While the heart is our primary blood pump, your leg muscles, when fit, will provide significant help in pushing blood back to the heart.

The heart gets stronger. Like any muscle, the heart's strength and effectiveness is increased through regular endurance exercise.

The lungs become more efficient in processing oxygen and inserting it into the blood

Adaptations: Our bodies are programmed to conserve resources by doing the smallest amount of work they can get away with. To improve, we must challenge the legs, the heart, the lungs, etc., in a gentle way, week by week. Here are only some of the resulting improvements:

- Mitochondria (energy powerhouse inside muscle cell) increase capacity and output.
- Mechanical efficiency of the foot is improved—more work with less effort.
- Legs keep you moving farther when tired—many positive adaptations are made.
- Muscle cells work as a team—using fewer resources, increasing performance, pumping blood back to heart.
- Mental concentration increases.
- Your spirit is unleashed as you find yourself improving.

Endorphins kill pain, make you feel good

Running at any pace, especially speed training, signals to your body that there will be some pain to kill. The natural response is to produce natural pain killers called endorphins. These hormones act as drugs that relax muscles, helping to deal with the damage and pain, while bestowing a good attitude—especially when you are tired after the run. Walking during the rest interval allows the endorphins to collect.

Gradually pushing up the workload

Even the most mature body is programmed to improve, when it is gradually introduced to a little more work, with enough rest afterward. Push too hard, or neglect the rest, and you'll see an increase in aches, pains and injury. When your training program is engineered for you, adjustments are made for legitimate problems and runners can stay injury-free most days, every year.

Stress + REST = Improvement

When running slightly faster than our realistic goal pace, muscle cells and tendons tend to break down from a greater workload. If the stress is not too much more than before, it will stimulate the body to make internal improvements. You see, our bodies are programmed to rebuild stronger than before when slightly overwhelmed. But there must be gentle and regular stress, followed by significant rest to promote this regeneration. Mature runners need to look at the Rest part of the equation very carefully.

Long Run, Hills
—the Key Elements

and Regularity

Endurance is produced by the long run

By gradually extending slow long runs, you train muscle cells to expand their capacity to utilize oxygen efficiently, sustain energy production, and in general, increase their capacity to get you farther down the road. The continued increase of the distance of long runs extends the reach of blood artery capillaries to deliver oxygen and improves the return of waste products so that the muscles can work at top capacity. In short, long runs bestow a better plumbing system, while improving muscle capacity. These improvements can increase the muscle response to speed training and racing.

Even when running very slowly, with liberal walk breaks, you build endurance by gradually increasing the distance of a regularly-scheduled long run. Start with the length of your current long run, and increase by .5 to 1 mile on each, or as noted in the following schedule:

- With a current long run of 1-2 miles, increase by half a mile every other week.

- When the long run reaches 4-6 miles, you can increase by 1 mile every other week.

- When the long run exceeds 9 miles, you can increase by 1-2 miles every 2 weeks, running half that amount on the non-long-run weekend.

- When the long run exceeds 17 miles, you can increase by 2-3 miles every 3 weeks, running 7-9 miles on the non-long-run weekend.

- Remember to run the long ones 2-3 min/mi slower than the "magic mile" time multiplied by 1.3. Example: magic mile time is 10:00, predicted marathon pace is 13 min/mile and long run training pace should be no faster than 15 min/mile. It is even better to slow down by another minute or two.

- Adjust pace for heat:
  50-60 year olds: 30 sec per mile slower for every 5 degrees above 60°F (20 sec/km for ea 2°C above 14°C)
  61-70 year olds: 35 sec per mile slower for every 5 degrees above 60°F (25 sec/km for ea 2°C above 14°C)
  71-80 year olds: 45 sec per mile slower for every 5 degrees above 60°F (33 sec/km for ea 2°C above 14°C)
  81-90 year olds: 60 sec per mile slower for every 5 degrees above 60°F (45 sec/km for ea 2°C above 14°C)
  91 + : Limit long runs to no more than 10-12 miles (15-20K) and follow formula for 81-90 year olds.

Strength through hill training

Build Strength…And More: Hill training has been used as the only form of speed training by a growing number of mature runners. It reduces the chance of certain types of speed training injuries. While you're improving your speed, you're strengthening the legs, and improving your ability to run hills in races. Hill training can be done year-round or as a gentle introduction to faster running.

A few hill repeats can be done on a short running day during the week, usually on Tuesday or Thursday. Start with a few of them and gradually increase by 1 each session. Don't sprint! The fastest pace of the first hill segment should be just a little faster than you would run during a training run. Veteran runners could increase the pace during each hill segment to about a 5K race pace when going over the top of the hill. Read the section below on hill running form.

The hill workout
- Walk for 5 minutes
- Jog and walk to a hill—about 10 minutes. Jog 1 minute and walk 1 minute (a longer warm-up is fine).
- Do 4 acceleration-gliders. These are listed in the "Drills" chapter (don't sprint).
- Reverse this warm-up as your warm down.

- Choose a hill with a gentle grade—steep hills often cause problems and bestow no benefit.
- Walk to the top of the hill. Then step off the length of your hill segment by walking down from the top:
    50 walking steps for beginners
    100-150 steps for those who have done a little speed work before
    150-200 steps for those who have done speed work, but not within the past 6 months
    200-300 steps for those who have been doing regular speed work
- Mark the place after you step it off. This is where each hill starts. Walk to the bottom of the hill.
- Finalize the warm-up: Run up the hill for 5 seconds, and then down for 5 seconds. Walk for 30-60 seconds. Repeat this 5-10 times.
- Walk for 3-4 minutes.
- Start your hill repeat workout. Run the first few steps of each hill acceleration at a jog, and then gradually pick up the turnover of the feet as you go up the hill.
- Get into a comfortable rhythm, so that you can gradually increase this rhythm or turnover (# of RPM's of feet and legs) as you go up the hill.
- Keep stride length short and keep shortening stride as you go up the hill.
- It's OK to huff and puff at the top of the hill, but don't let the legs get over extended, or feel exhausted.
- Run over the top of the hill by at least 10 steps.
- Jog back to the top of the hill and walk down to recover between the hills. Walk as much as you need for complete recovery after each hill.

Hill running form
- Start with a comfortable stride—fairly short.
- As you go up the hill, shorten the stride.
- Touch lightly with your feet.

- Maintain a body posture that is perpendicular to the horizontal (upright, not leaning forward or back).
- Pick up the turnover of your feet as you go up and over the top.
- Keep adjusting stride so that the leg muscles don't tighten up—you want them as resilient as possible.
- Relax as you go over the top of the hill, and glide (or coast) a bit on the downside.

Hill training strengthens lower legs and improves running form

The incline of the hill forces your legs to work harder as you go up. The extra work up the incline and the faster turnover, builds strength. By taking an easy walk between the hills, and an easy day afterward, the lower leg muscles become stronger. Over several months, the improved strength allows you to support your body weight farther forward on your feet. An extended range of motion of the ankle and achilles tendon results in a "bonus" extension of the foot forward, with no increase in effort. You will run faster without working harder. What a deal!

Running faster on hills in races

Once you train yourself to run with efficient hill form, you'll run faster with increased turnover on the hill workouts. This prepares you to do the same in races. You won't run quite as fast in a race as in your workouts. But through hill training you can run faster than you used to run up the same hill on a race course.

Race hill technique is the same as in workouts: keep shortening stride as you move up the hill. Monitor your respiration rate: don't huff and puff more than you were doing on the flat. As runners improve their hill technique in races, they find that a shorter and quicker stride reduces effort while increasing speed—with no increase in breathing.

Note: on your long runs and easy running days, just jog up hills; don't run faster up the hill. If your breathing is increasing on a hill, reduce effort and stride length until your respiration is as it was on the flat ground.

Downhill form

- Run light on your feet.
- Maintain an average stride—don't over stride.
- Keep feet low to the ground.
- Let gravity pull you down the hill.
- Turnover of the feet will pick up.
- Try to glide (or coast) quickly down the hill.

Biggest mistakes: too long a stride, bouncing too much

Mature runners can dramatically increase recovery time when they let their stride increase by even 1 or 2 inches too long. Downhill speed can get out of control. If you are bouncing more than an inch or 2 off the ground, you run the risk of pounding your feet, having to use your quads to slow down (producing soreness) and creating hamstring soreness due to over stride. The best indicator of over stride is having tight hamstrings (big muscle behind your upper leg) after a hill workout.

Regularity

Maintain current endurance by running two 30 minute runs, every other day (i.e., Tues and Thurs)

A half hour run on Tuesday and Thursday will maintain the endurance gained on the weekend. This is the minimum and also results in the lowest injury rate. If you are already running more than this, without aches and pains, you can continue if you wish. As you will see in *Year Round Plan*, *Galloway's Book on Running* 2ND Edition, *Marathon* and others, more training is needed to achieve most of the time goals.

Mature and Faster!

Getting faster requires extra work—with more injury risk

Most mature runners hardly ever run speed work. It is common knowledge that speed training dramatically increases the chance of injury. Even a small amount over your speed limit, can result in longer recovery and lingering soreness not experienced after longer and slower runs. If you decide to train for a time goal, schedule a series of workouts that start at your current level of performance, pushing only a little harder in each workout. It is also crucial that you reduce intensity after speed sessions so that your performance systems can rebound and rebuild. Gradual and gentle increases are always better because you are more likely to sustain a continuous and long-term improvement.

Introducing the body to speed through "drills"

Mature runners will further reduce injury risk of speed work by regularly doing the two drills that are detailed in the "Drills" chapter: Cadence Drills (CD) & Acceleration-Gliders (Acg). These drills can be done as a warm-up before speed sessions and in place of a speed session when the muscles feel like they may not be ready for a full speed workout. Warning: don't push the muscles or stride too far—stay within your range of motion and exertion.

The CD drill helps to improve the number of steps you take per minute. The Acg drill provides a very gentle introduction to speed work, in very short segments, and maintains the adaptations. Most of the running during the conditioning period is at an easy pace. These drills can be done in the middle of a short run, once or twice a week, and will improve mechanics, get the muscles ready for the heavier demands of speed training and initiate internal physiological changes in the muscles—with very little risk of injury. I've heard of major time improvements from mature runners who do no other form of speed training than these drills.

A gentle increase causes a manageable breakdown

The weekly speed workout starts with a few speed repetitions, with rest between each. As the number of repetitions increase each session, your body is pushed slightly beyond what it did during the previous one. In each workout, your muscle fibers get tired as they reach the previous maximum workload, and continue like motivated slaves to keep you running the pace assigned. In every session some are pushed beyond their capacity. Often, pain and fatigue are not felt during the workout. But within one or two days there are usually sore muscles and tendons, and a general sensation of overall tiredness. Even walking may not feel smooth for a day or two after a speed session that is run too hard—a clear sign that you went too fast or did not insert enough rest for the conditions.

The damage
Looking inside the cell at the end of a hard workout, you'll see damage:

- Tears in the muscle cell membrane
- The mitochondria (that process the energy inside the cell) are swollen.
- There's a significant lowering of the muscle stores of glycogen (the energy supply needed in speed work).
- Waste products from exertion, bits of bone and muscle tissue and other bio junk, can be found.
- Sometimes, there are small tears in the blood vessels and arteries, and blood leaks into the muscles

The damage stimulates the muscles, tendons, etc. to rebuild stronger and better than before
Your body is programmed to get better when it is pushed beyond its current limits. A slight increase is better than a greater increase because the repair can be done relatively quickly.

Mature runners need to ensure enough rest afterward
Two days after a speed session, if the muscles have had enough rest, you'll see some improvements:

- Waste has been removed.
- Thicker cell membranes can handle more work without breaking down.

- The mitochondria have increased in size and number so that they can process more energy next time.
- The damage to the blood system has been repaired.
- Over several months, after adapting to a continued series of small increases, more capillaries (tiny fingers of the blood system) are produced. This improves and expands the delivery of oxygen and nutrients and provides a better withdrawal of waste products.

At any age....

These are only some of the many adaptations made by the incredible human body when we exercise: bio-mechanics, nervous system, strength, muscle efficiency and more. Internal psychological improvements follow the physical ones. Mind, body and spirit are becoming a team, improving health and performance. An added benefit is a positive attitude.

Quality rest is crucial: 48 hours between workouts

Most runners over 45 run better when they run every other day and do no running on the day between. On rest days, it's also important to avoid exercises that strenuously use the calf muscle, ankle and achilles tendon (stair machines, step aerobics, spinning out of the saddle) for the 48 hour period between running workouts. Mature runners must be particularly sensitive to other aches and pains from your individual "weak links." Walking is usually a great exercise for a rest day. There are several other good exercises in the "Cross Training" section of this book. Water running on non-running days has helped many runners improve significantly. As long as you are not continuing to stress the calf, most alternative exercises are fine. Avoid any activity that seems to sustain fatigue in the calf muscle, or activate aches and pains in your "weak link" areas.

Beware of junk miles

Mature runners often compromise their running goals and orthopedic health by "sneaking in" a few easy miles on a day that should be a day off from running. With each decade of age, the 48 hour recovery period between runs becomes more important. These short runs are called "junk miles" because they don't improve conditioning—and they interfere with muscle recovery.

Regularity

To maintain the adaptations, you must regularly run, about every 2 days. To maintain the speed improvements mentioned in this book, you should do the speed workouts listed in the appropriate training schedule in one of my other books or website *(www.Jeff Galloway.com)*. It is OK to delay a workout every once in a while, but missing 2 workouts in a row will result in a slight loss of your current performance capability. The longer you wait, the more careful a mature runner must be when starting again.

"Muscle memory"

Your neuro-muscular system remembers the patterns of muscle exertion which you have done regularly, over an extended period of time. Mature runners who've been running for 10 or more years can do very little running on their short "maintenance" days and retain their conditioning for a long time.

Tip: Cramped for time? Just run for 10 minutes

Let's say that you don't have 30 minutes on an easy day. It is much better to run for 10 minutes on these days, than to let 3 or more days go by without a run. If you are doing speed training and are in a time bind, do a few accelerations during the 10-15 minute run, and you'll maintain most of your adaptations.

Aerobic running is done during long runs

Aerobic means "in the presence of oxygen." This is the type of running you do when you feel "slow" and comfortable. When running aerobically, your muscles can get enough oxygen from the blood to process the energy in the cells (burning fat in most cases). The minimal waste products produced during aerobic running can be easily removed, with no lingering build-up. Mature runners should spend at least 90% of their time in the "aerobic zone."

Speed training gets you into the anaerobic zone: producing an oxygen debt

Anaerobic running is running too fast or too long for you, on that day. At some point in the workout, when you reach your current limit, the muscles can't get enough oxygen to burn the most efficient fuel—fat. So, they shift to the limited supply of stored sugar: glycogen. The waste products from this fuel pile up quickly in the cells, tightening the muscles and causing you to breathe heavily. This is called an oxygen debt. If you keep running for too long in this anaerobic state, you will have to slow down significantly or stop. But if you are running for a realistic time goal, and are pacing yourself correctly, you should only be running anaerobically for a short period of time at the end of each workout and race. Mature runners need to limit the time they run in an anaerobic state because too much time in this zone will require a much longer recovery.

The anaerobic threshold

As you increase the quantity of your speed repetitions, you push back your current anaerobic threshold. This means that you can run a bit farther than before—each week, at the same pace, without extreme huffing and puffing. Your muscles can move your body farther and faster without going to exhaustion. Each speed workout pushes you a little bit further into the anaerobic zone. To run faster at any age, you will have to learn how to deal with an oxygen debt. Speed training teaches the body that it can go farther before going anaerobic, how to deal with the discomfort this produces and how to keep going when the muscles are tight and tired. It also tells you that you don't have to give up on performance when in this state. Learning how to keep going when anaerobic is crucial if you want to run faster.

More rest between speed repetitions

I've found that mature runners can get about the same benefit from speed workouts as younger runners—even when taking more rest between repetitions. See the recommendations on page 36 in this book.

The talk test: How aerobic are you?

- You're aerobic...if you can talk for as long as you want with minimal huffing & puffing (h & p).
- You are mostly aerobic...if you can talk for 30 sec + then must h & p for no more than 10 sec.
- You are approaching anaerobic threshold...if you can only talk for 10 sec or less, then h & p for 10+ sec
- You're anaerobic...if you can't talk more than a few words, and are mostly huffing and puffing.

Fast twitch vs. slow twitch muscle fibers

We are born with a combination of 2 types of muscle fibers. Those with a high percentage of fast-twitchers can run fast for a short distance and then become very tired. Fast twitch fibers are designed to burn the stored sugar in your muscles: glycogen. This is the fuel we use during the first 15 minutes of exercise (and during speed work), and it can produce a lot of waste product, such as lactic acid. If we run even a little too fast at the beginning of a run, the muscles will become very tight and tired very quickly. You will huff and puff and feel increasingly uncomfortable. This fuel is in limited supply for distance running.

If you have a higher percentage of slow twitch fibers, you won't be able to run as fast at first, but can keep going for longer distances. Slow twitch fibers burn fat, which is a fuel that is very efficient and produces little waste product. Long runs will not only condition the slow twitch fibers to work at top capacity as they efficiently burn fat. As you increase the length of the long ones, you'll train some of your fast twitch fibers to burn fat as fuel—and to function as slow-twitchers.

Once the starting pace of a race or a workout is controlled (and also the ego), fast runners develop a mix of fast- and slow-twitchers to do the work of running. They also find that they don't get exhausted at the end. It is the slow pace and walk breaks that keep you in the aerobic (or fat-burning) zone. At this reduced level of performance, you can burn fat and push back the endurance limit.

Are you working too hard toward a time goal?

Mature runners who have time goals can get too focused on running faster almost every run. This often results in injury. One of the first signs is increased stress associated with running, often resulting in motivation problems. At the first sign of these symptoms, reduce mileage and let mind and body get back together again:

- Running is not as enjoyable.
- You don't look forward to your runs.
- When you say something to others about your running, the statements are often negative.
- The negativity can permeate other areas of your life.
- You look on running as work instead of play.

The personal growth of speed training

- If you keep from over-training during speed sessions, you'll tend to look forward to them.
- Instead of looking just at the times in your races, embrace the life lessons that can come from the journey of an extended speed training program.
- Most of your runs must have some fun in them, to help you through the challenges.
- Even after a hard workout, focus on how good you feel afterward.
- At any age, the satisfaction from overcoming adversity is personally empowering.
- Try to find some fun in very session.

The reality of a speed training program is that you'll have more setbacks than victories. But you will learn more from the setbacks which will make you a stronger runner—and a stronger person. Confronting challenges is initially tough, but leads you to some of the great treasure of the improvement process. Above all, remember that if you are injured from fast running, you will lose the good feelings from every run. So, be very careful and stop the workout at the first sign of an injury.

The Drills — to Make Running Faster and Easier

All runners benefit from the following drills. Even if you never want to run any faster, these will help you run more efficiently. Those who want to run faster will find that the drills can be a substitute for speed work on days when the legs aren't fully ready for the challenge.

The following drills have helped thousands of runners run more efficiently and faster. Each one develops different capabilities, and each rewards the individual for running smoother, reducing impact, using momentum and increasing the cadence or turnover of feet and legs. With each drill, you're teaching yourself to move more directly and easily down the road, without the stress incurred by speed training.

No aches...no pains

If the leg muscles or tendons are sore the next day after these drills, you did them too hard. Reduce stride length next time to eliminate the aggravation. Each drill should be run gently and within your mechanical range of motion. Never push against your limits on these.

When?

These should be done on a non-long run day. It is fine, however, to do them as part of your warm-up, before a race or a speed workout. Many runners have also told me that the drills are a nice way to break up an average run that otherwise might be called "boring."

Cadence Drill (CD)

This is a gentle drill that helps you run smoother and easier. By doing CD's regularly, you pull all the elements of good running form together at the same time. One drill a week will help you step lightly, while you increase the number of steps you take per minute. This will help you run faster, with less effort.

1. Warm up by walking for 5 minutes, and running and walking very gently for 10 minutes.
2. Start jogging slowly for 1-2 minutes, and then time yourself for 30 seconds. During this half minute, count the number of times your left foot touches.
3. Walk or jog slowly for a minute or so.
4. On the 2nd CD, your mission is to increase the count by 1 or 2.
5. Repeat this 3-7 more times. Each time trying to increase by 1-2 additional counts.

In the process of improving turnover, the body's internal monitoring system coordinates a series of adaptations which make the feet, legs, nerve system and timing mechanism work together as an efficient team:

- Your foot touches quickly and lightly.
- Inefficient motions of the foot and leg are reduced or eliminated.

- Less effort is spent on pushing up so you can move forward.
- You stay lower to the ground.
- The ankle becomes more efficient.
- Ache and pain areas are not overused.

Note: At the beginning of each of these, start with a clean slate. Whatever the first count is, try to keep increasing by one additional on each successive one.

Acceleration-Glider Drills (Acg)

This drill is a very easy and gentle form of speed play, or fartlek. By doing it regularly, you develop a range of speeds, with the muscle conditioning to move smoothly from one to the next. The greatest benefit is learning how to "glide," or coast, off your momentum.

1. Do these drills on a non-long-run day, in the middle of a shorter run, or as a warm-up for a speed session or a race.
2. Warm up with at least half a mile of easy running.
3. Many runners do the cadence drill just after the easy warm-up, and then the acceleration-gliders (These can be done separately from the turnover drill, if desired).
4. Run 4-8 of each.
5. Do this at least once a week.
6. No sprinting—never run all-out.

After teaching this drill at my one-day running schools and weekend retreats for years, I have observed that most people learn better through practice when they work on the concepts (rather than the details) of the drill. I hope you can join us at one of these sessions. In the meantime, just get out there and try them! Remember—no aches and pains.

Gliding. This is the most important concept. This is like coasting off the momentum of a downhill run. You can do some of your gliders running down a hill if you want, but it is important to do at least 2 of them on the flat land.

Do this every week. As in the turnover drills, the regularity of the drill is very important. If you're like most runners, you won't glide very far at first. Regular practice will help you learn how to glide farther and farther.

Don't sweat the small stuff. I've included a general guideline of how many steps to do with each part of the drill, but don't worry about getting an exact number of steps.

Smooth transition. Do this between each of the components. Each time you "shift gears" you are using the momentum of the current mode to start you into the next mode. Don't make a sudden and abrupt change, but have a gentle shift between modes.

Here's how it's done:
- Start by jogging very slowly for about 15 steps.
- Then, jog faster for about 15 steps, increasing to a regular running pace for you.
- Now, over the next 15 steps, gradually increase the speed to your current race pace.
- Now, it's time to glide, or coast. Allow yourself to gradually slow down to a jog using momentum as long as you can. At first you may only glide for 4 or 5 steps. As the months go by you will get up to 20, then 30 and beyond....you're gliding!

Overall purpose: As you do this drill, every week, your form will become smoother at each mode of running. Congratulations! You are learning how to keep moving at a fairly fast pace without using much energy. This is the main object of the drill.

There will be some weeks when you will glide longer than others— don't worry about this. By doing this drill regularly, you will find yourself coasting or gliding down the smallest of inclines, and even for 10-20 yards on the flat, on a regular basis. Gliding conserves energy, reduces soreness and fatigue, and helps you maintain a faster pace in races.

Your Journal—for Planning, Evaluation and Motivation

This is your book

Yes, you are writing a book, which may include areas other than running. Whether you want to improve or not, the journal helps you organize your running week in advance and collect the details of your run—and your day—for that day. Later, you can review after successes or disappointments, and often find reasons for either. If we don't look at the reasons behind our negative running history, we will have a tendency to repeat it.

Computer logs, training journals, notebooks

There are a growing number of software products that allow you to sort through information more quickly. In working with a company (PC Coach) to incorporate my training program, I discovered that this format speeds up the search for needed information. As you set up your own codes and sections, you can pick data that are important to you, sort it to see trends, and plan ahead. Some software (including mine) allows you to download data from a heart monitor or GPS watch.

Most runners use notebook products. My *Galloway's Training Journal* has 52 weeks of entries with spaces for the key data items I've found significant. Simple log books can be made from school notebooks or calendars. The best product is one that you will use regularly.

The planning process

1. Look over your chosen schedule from *Testing Yourself, Marathon, Year Round Plan, Galloway's Book on Running*, 2nd Edition, or *Half-Marathon*.
2. Write down the key races and major workouts on the appropriate weeks in your journal. Take a hi-lighter, etc., to make these weeks stand out.
3. Write down the assigned workouts for each day of each week for the next 8 weeks—in pencil.
4. Look at each of the next 8 weeks quickly to make sure you don't have any trips, meetings or family responsibilities that require adjusting the workouts.

5. Each week, add another week's workouts in pencil, and note any changes in your travel schedule.
6. Each week, look ahead carefully at the next 2 weeks to ensure that the workouts are adjusted to your real life schedule.

The data recording

1. As soon as you can, after a run, write these results in your journal:
   - mileage
   - repetitions—times
   - aches or pains
   - pace
   - rest interval
   - problems

In addition, you may also record:

Time of run:

Total Time running:

Weather:

Temperature:

Precipitation:

Humidity:

Walk-Run frequency:

Any special segments of the run (speed, hills, race, etc.)

Running companion:

Terrain:

How did you feel (1-10)

Comments:

2. Go back over the list again and fill in more details such as emotional responses, changes in energy or blood sugar level, and location of places where you had aches and pains—even if they went away during the run. You are looking for patterns of items that could indicate injury, blood sugar problems, lingering fatigue, etc.

Your morning pulse can help you monitor over-training

Recording morning pulse immediately upon waking

1. As soon as you are conscious, but before you have thought much about anything, count your pulse rate for a minute. Record it before you forget it. If you don't have your journal by your bed, then keep a pen and paper handy.

2. It is natural for there to be some fluctuations, based upon the time you wake up, how long you have been awake, etc. But after several weeks and months, these will balance themselves out. The ideal situation would be to catch the pulse at the instant that you are awake, before the shock of an alarm clock, thoughts of work stress, etc.

3. After 2 weeks or so of readings, you can establish a baseline morning pulse. Take out the top 2 high readings and then average the readings.

4. The average is your guide. If the rate is 5% higher than your average, take an easy day. When the rate is 10% higher, and there is no reason for this (you woke up from an exciting dream, medication, infection, etc.), then your muscles may be tired indeed. Take the day off if you have a walk-run scheduled for that day.

5. If your pulse stays high for more than a week, call your doctor to see if there is a reason for this (medication, hormones, metabolic changes, etc.)

The Principles of Great Running Form

After having individually analyzed thousands of runners in my running schools and weekend retreats, I've found that most are running very close to their ideal efficiency. Overall, try to run easier and smoother. The mistakes are seldom major. But, a series of small ones can result in slower times, aches, pains and sometimes injuries. By making a few minor adjustments, most runners can feel better and run faster.

When mature runners make a small mistake in stride length, extra bounce, etc., it can greatly increase recovery time. Before I detail these common problems, let's look at some principles of running form for distances longer than half a mile.

Inertia is our friend

The primary mission for distance runners is to maintain momentum. Very little strength is needed to run—even when running fast for short races like the 800 meters. During the first hundred meters, you'll get your body into the motion and rhythm for your run. After that, the best strategy is to conserve energy while maintaining that momentum. To reduce fatigue, aches and pains, your right brain, helped by muscle memory, intuitively fine-tunes your mechanics and motion to minimize effort.

Humans have many bio-mechanical adaptations working for them, which have been made more efficient over more than a million years of walking and running. The anatomical running efficiency of the human body originates in the ankle and achilles tendon—which I treat as a unit. This is no average body part, however, but an extremely sophisticated system of levers, springs, balancing devices and more. Bio-mechanics experts believe that this degree of development was not needed for walking. When our ancient ancestors had to run to survive, the ankle/achilles adapted to long trips on foot by evolving into a masterpiece of bio-engineering.

Through several weeks of regular running and drills, you can maximize use of the achilles and ankle so that a very little amount of muscle work produces a quicker, more efficient forward movement. During the first few sessions your legs may be a little sore. But as you get in better shape, with improved endurance, you'll find yourself going farther and faster with little or no increased effort. Other muscle groups offer support and help to fine-tune the process. When you feel aches and pains that might be due to the way you run, going back to the minimal use of the ankle and achilles tendon can often leave you feeling smooth and efficient very quickly. This may also reduce or eliminate the source of pain.

Mature runners usually benefit from:

- Shuffling feet lower to the ground
- Short stride reduces aggravation of tendons and muscles dramatically
- Light touch of the feet
- Working on a quicker turnover of feet and legs (through CD drill in last chapter)

Mature runners should avoid:
- Lengthening stride
- Bouncing off the ground
- Too much pounding on the feet

Three negative results of inefficient form:

1. Fatigue from extraneous motions becomes so severe that it takes much longer to recover.
2. Muscles or tendons are pushed so far beyond their limits that they break down and become injured—or just hurt.
3. The experience is so negative that the desire to run is reduced, resulting in burnout.

Wobbling: It all starts with general fatigue that stresses your weak links. For example, when your muscles are beyond their limits at the end of a workout or a race, and you keep pushing to maintain pace, your body will use other muscles and tendons to keep you going. You start to "wobble" as these alternatives are not designed to do the job. The longer you "wobble," the more likely you are to produce an injury.

Stride extension when tired: There are several instincts that can hurt us. When tired, for example, many runners subconsciously extend stride length to maintain pace. This may work for a while, at the expense of the quads, hamstrings, and several other components that are over-stressed. It is always better, when you feel even a slight aggravation at the end of a run, to cut stride, and get back into a smooth motion. It's OK to push through tiredness when running smoothly as long as you are not feeling pain in any area. But if this means extending stride or wobbling (which aggravates your weak links), it's not OK.

No knee lift: Avoid the temptation to lift knees to maintain speed. This produces sore quads, hips and groin pain.

Be sensitive and avoid irritation: I don't suggest that everyone should try to create perfect form. Try to be aware of your form problems, and make changes to keep them from producing aches and pains. This will allow you to run smoother, reduce fatigue, and over time will help you to run faster.

Relaxed muscles—especially at the end of the run

Overall, the running motion should feel smooth, and there should be no tension in your neck, back, shoulders or legs. Even during the last half mile of a hard workout or race, try to maintain the three main elements of good form, and you'll stay relaxed: upright posture, feet low to the ground and relaxed stride. You should not try to push through tightness and pain. Adjust your form to reduce aches and recovery time.

The big three: posture, stride and bounce

In thousands of individual running form consultations, I've discovered that when runners have problems, they tend to occur in these three areas. Often the problems are like a signature—tending to be very specific to the areas that you overuse, because of your unique movement patterns. By making a few small changes in your running form, you can reduce or eliminate the source of the problems, which is also the source of the pain.

I. POSTURE

Good running posture is actually good body posture. The head is naturally balanced over the shoulders, which are aligned over the hips. As the foot comes underneath and all of these elements are in balance, little energy is needed to prop up the body, and keep it moving. By maintaining good form, you don't have to work harder to pull a wayward body back from a wobble or inefficient motion.

Forward lean—the most common mistake

The posture errors tend to be mostly due to a forward lean, especially when we are tired. The head wants to get to the finish as soon as possible, but the legs can't go any faster. A common tendency at the end of a speed session is to lean with the head. In races, this results in more than a few falls around the finish line. A forward lean will often concentrate fatigue, soreness and tightness in the lower back or neck. Bio-mechanics experts note that a forward lean will reduce stride length, causing a slowdown or an increase in effort.

It all starts with the head. When the neck muscles are relaxed, the head can naturally seek an alignment that is balanced on the shoulders. If there is tension in the neck, or soreness afterward, the head is usually leaning too far forward. This triggers a more general upper body imbalance in which the head and chest are suspended slightly ahead of the hips and feet. Sometimes, headaches result from this postural problem. Ask a running companion to tell you if and when your head is too far forward, or leaning down. This usually occurs at the end of a tiring run. The ideal position of the head is mostly upright, with your eyes focused about 30-40 yards ahead of you.

Note: There are 2 strength exercises, mentioned in my books, which help maintain good posture: "arm running" and "the crunch."

Hips

The hips are the other major postural component that can easily get out of alignment. A runner with this problem, when observed from the side, will have the butt behind the rest of the body. When the pelvis area is shifted back, the legs are not allowed to go through their ideal range of motion, and the stride length is shortened. This produces a slower pace, even when spending significant effort. Many runners tend to hit harder on their heels when their hips are shifted back—but this is not always the case.

A backward lean is rare

It is rare for runners to lean back, but it happens. In my experience, this is usually due to a structural problem in the spine or hips. If you do this, and you're having pain in the neck, back or hips, you should see an orthopedist that specializes in the back. One symptom is excessive shoe wear on the back of the heel, but there are other reasons why you may show this kind of wear.

Posture correction: "Puppet on a string"

The best correction I've found to postural problems has been this mental image exercise: imagine that you are a puppet on a string.

In other words, you're suspended from above like a puppet—from the head and each side of the shoulders. In this way, your head lines up above the shoulders, the hips come directly underneath, and the feet naturally touch lightly, directly underneath. It won't hurt anyone to do the "puppet" several times during a run.

It helps to combine this image with a deep breath. About every 4-5 minutes, as you start to run after a walk break for example, take a deep, lower lung breath, straighten up and say "I'm a puppet." Then imagine that you don't have to spend energy maintaining this upright posture, because the strings attached from above keep you on track. As you continue to do this, you reinforce good posture, and the behavior can become a good habit.

Upright posture not only allows you to stay relaxed, you will probably improve stride length. When you lean forward, you'll be cutting your stride to stay balanced. When you straighten up, you'll receive a stride bonus of an inch or so, without any increase in energy. Note: don't try to increase stride length. When it happens naturally, you won't feel it—you'll just run faster.

An oxygen dividend—and no more side pain!
Breathing improves when you straighten up. A leaning body can't get ideal use out of the lower lungs. This can cause side pain. When you run upright the lower lungs can receive adequate air, maximize oxygen absorption and reduce the chance of side pain.

II. FEET LOW TO THE GROUND
The most efficient stride is a shuffle with feet right next to the ground. As long as you pick your foot up enough to avoid stumbling over a rock or uneven pavement, stay low to the ground. Most runners don't need to get more than 1 inch clearance, even when running fast. As you increase speed and ankle action, you will come off the ground a bit more than this. Again, don't try to increase stride; let this happen naturally.

Your ankle combined with your achilles tendon will act as a spring, moving you forward with each running step. If you stay low to the ground, very little effort is required. Through this "shuffling" technique, running becomes almost automatic. When runners err on bounce, they try to push off too hard. This usually results in extra effort spent, lifting the body off the ground. You can think of this as energy wasted in the air—energy that could be used to run faster.

The other negative force that penalizes a higher bounce is gravity. The higher you rise, the harder you fall. Each additional bounce off the ground delivers a lot more impact on feet and legs. During speed sessions, races and long runs, more bounce produces aches, pains and injuries.

The correction for too much bounce: Light touch
The ideal foot "touch" should be so light that you don't usually feel yourself pushing off or landing. This means that your foot stays low to the ground and goes though an efficient and natural motion. Instead of trying to overcome gravity, you get in synch with it. If your foot "slaps" when you run, you will definitely improve with a lighter touch.

Here's a "light touch drill": During the middle of a run, time yourself for 20 seconds. Focus on one item: touching so softly that you don't hear your feet. Earplugs are not allowed for this drill. Imagine that you are running on thin ice or through a bed of hot coals. Do several of these 20 second touches, becoming quieter and quieter. You should feel very little impact on your feet as you do this drill. This drill is particularly beneficial when you are tired.

III. STRIDE LENGTH
Studies have shown that as runners get faster, the stride length shortens. This clearly shows that the key to faster and more efficient running is increased cadence (quicker turnover) of feet and legs. A major cause of aches, pains and injuries is a stride length that is too long. When in doubt, it is always better to err on the side of having a shorter stride.

Mature runners will naturally experience a tightening of the running muscles. This is not usually a problem, only a reality. As the body adapts to the running motion, tightening of certain body mechanics will make running more efficient, which you're programmed to do. Don't try to "stretch out" a muscle that is tired after a run. After-run stretching produces a lot of injuries.

Don't lift your knees!
Even most of the world class distance runners don't have a high knee lift. When your knees are carried too high, you tend to over-use the quadriceps (front of the thigh), resulting in a stride that is too long to be efficient. This often produces sore quads for the next day or two.

Don't kick out too far in front of you!
If you watch the natural movement of the leg, it will kick forward slightly as the foot gently moves forward in the running motion and then comes underneath to contact the ground. Let this be a natural motion that produces no tightness in the muscles behind the lower or upper leg.

Tightness or pain in the front of the shin, behind the knee or in the hamstring (back of the thigh) are signs that you are kicking too far forward, and reaching out too far. Correct this by staying low to the ground, shortening the stride and lightly touching the ground.

"Motivational training gives you control over your attitude"

Mental Toughness

Left brain vs. right brain

The brain has two hemispheres that are separated and don't interconnect. The logical left brain does our business activities, trying to steer us into pleasure and away from discomfort. The creative and intuitive right side is an unlimited source of solutions to problems, connecting us to hidden strengths.

As we accumulate stress, the left brain sends us a stream of messages: "slow down," "stop," "this isn't your day" and even philosophical messages like, "Why are you doing this?" We are all capable of staying on track and pushing to a higher level of performance—even when the left brain tells us these things.

The first step in taking command over motivation is to ignore the left brain unless there is a legitimate reason of health or safety (very rare), or, if you are running a lot faster than you are ready to run. Here are three successful strategies for dealing with the left brain, and letting the right brain solve problems to you realize your potential.

Three strategies for staying mentally tough: Rehearsal, magic words, dirty tricks

These allow the right side of the brain to work on solutions to current problems. By preparing mentally for the challenges you expect, you will empower the right brain to deal with the problems and to tap into the inner sources of strength: the essence of mental toughness. You're installing a software program that finds a way to get the job done.

I. Rehearsing success:

Rehearsals develop patterns of thinking that get you in the groove for the behaviors you will need when challenged. In a tough situation, you don't want to have to think about the stress or the challenge—you want to get the job done. Instead of concentrating on the problem, you should work on the solution. Take the actions necessary to deal with the problem. "Challenge rehearsals" will format your brain for a series of behaviors, which can become automatic, and lead you to the finish line. By repeating the pattern and adjusting, you'll revise it for real life. It can become more consistent and you will feel the confidence of using the same routine when you face the challenge in real life. Let's learn by doing.

Drill # 1
Getting out the door after a hard day

1. State your desired outcome: To be running from my house after a hard day.

2. Detail the challenge: Low blood sugar and fatigue, a stream of negative messages, need to do family activities, overwhelming desire to feel relaxed.

3. Break up the challenge into a series of actions, which lead you through the mental barriers, none of which is challenging to the left brain.

- You're driving home at the end of the day, knowing that it is your workout day but you have no energy.
- Your left brain says: "You're too tired. Take the day off. You don't have the energy to run."
- So you say to the left brain: "I'm not going to exercise. I'll put on some comfortable shoes and clothes, eat and drink, get food preparation going for dinner, and feel relaxed."
- You're in your room, putting on comfortable clothes and shoes (they just happen to be used for running).
- You're drinking coffee (tea, diet cola, etc) and eating a good tasting energy snack, as you get the food prepared to go into the oven.
- Stepping outside, you check on the weather.
- You're walking to the edge of your block to see what the neighbors are doing.
- As you cross the street, you're on your way.
- The endorphins are kicking in, you feel good. You want to continue.

4. Rehearse the situation over and over, fine-tuning it so that it becomes integrated into the way you think and act—and reflects the specific situation that you will encounter in your challenge.

5. Finish by mentally enjoying the after-run glow, with the desired outcome. You feel good: great attitude, vitality, and you're relaxed. You are enjoying the sense of accomplishment for the rest of the evening.

Drill # 2
Getting out the door early in the morning

Almost everyone has "those mornings" when the gravity is greater than normal when the alarm goes off.

1. State your desired outcome: To be walking and running away from the house early in the morning.

2. Detail the challenge: Desire to lie in bed, no desire to exert yourself so early, the stress of the alarm clock, and having to think about what to do next when the brain isn't working very fast.

3. Break up the challenge into a series of actions, which lead you through the mental barriers, none of which is challenging to the left brain.

- The night before, lay out your running clothes and shoes, near your coffee pot, so that you don't have to think.
- Set your alarm, and say to yourself over and over, "Alarm off, feet on the floor, to the coffee pot" or, "Alarm, floor, coffee." As you repeat this, you visualize doing each action without thinking. By repeating it, you lull yourself to sleep. You have also been programming yourself for taking action the next morning.
- The alarm goes off. You shut it off, put feet on the floor, and you head to the coffee pot—all without thinking.
- You're putting on one piece of clothing at a time, sipping coffee, never thinking about exercise.

- With coffee cup in hand, you walk out the door to see what the weather is like.
- Sipping coffee, you walk to edge of your block or property to see what the neighbors are doing.
- Putting coffee down, you cross the street, and you have made the break!
- The endorphins are kicking in, you feel good. You want to continue.

4. Rehearse the situation over and over, fine-tuning it so that it becomes integrated into the way you think and act—and reflects the specific situation that you will encounter in your challenge situation.

5. Finish by mentally enjoying the after-run glow, with the desired outcome. You feel good: great attitude, vitality, and you're relaxed. You are enjoying the sense of accomplishment for the rest of the day.

Drill # 3
Pushing past the fatigue point where you tend to slow down

Situation: You're into a hard workout or race, and you are really tired. Your left brain is telling you that you can't reach your goal today. "Just slow down a little, there are other days to work hard."
Evaluation: Is there is a real medical reason why you can't run as projected? If there is, back off and conserve—there will be another day. If the temperature or weather presents challenges, adjust. For example, slow down for every 5 degrees of temperature increase above 60°F.
Make a commitment: In most cases, when the temperature is below 60°F, the problem is simple: you are not willing to push through the discomfort. The most effective way of getting tough mentally is to keep going as you gradually push back your limits. Speed training programs do this naturally as you gradually increase the number of repetitions. As you add to the length of your run,

number of speed sessions, etc., the body and the mind work together to keep you going when you are challenged.

Don't quit! Mental toughness starts by not giving up. Just ignore the negative messages and stay focused to the finish of your run. If you've trained adequately, hang on and keep going.

In your speed workouts, practice the following drill. Fine-tune this so that when you run your goal race, you will have a strategy for staying mentally tough.

The scene:

You're getting very tired, you'd really like to call it quits, or at least slow down significantly.

Quick strategies:
- Break up the remaining workout or race into segments that you know you can do:
- 1 more minute: Run for one minute, then reduce pace slightly (or walk) for 10-20 seconds, then say, "One more minute," again, and again.
- 10 more steps: Run about 10 steps, take several easy steps, then say "Ten more steps."
- One more step: Keep saying this over and over—you'll get there

Take some shuffle breaks
- Reduce the tension on your leg muscles and feet by shuffling for a few strides every 1-2 minutes. By practicing "the shuffle," you'll find that you don't slow down much at all—while your muscles feel better.

Lap by lap, mile by mile
- In the workouts, start each lap saying to your self, "Just one more," (even if you have 4 to go) or, "I'll just run half a lap." You'll run the whole thing. You're negotiating with your left brain.
- In a track race say, "One more lap," or, "One more half lap," or, "Just around the curve." In a road race say, "One more mile," or, "One more block," or, "Just around the curve."

- When you are getting close to the end and really feel like you can't keep going, say to yourself, "I am tough," or, "I can endure," or, "Yes I can," or, "One more step."

II. Magic Words

Even the most motivated person has sections during a tough workout or race when he or she wants to quit. By using a successful brainwashing technique, you can pull yourself through these negative thoughts and feel like a champion at the end. On these days, you have not only reached the finish line, you've overcome challenges to get there.

Think back to the problems that you faced in your tough workouts or races. These are the ones that are most likely to challenge you again. As you go through a series of speed sessions and long runs, you will confront just about every problem you will face in the race. Go back in your memory bank and pull out instances when you started to lose motivation due to these, but finished and overcame the challenge.

Galloway's Magic Words: "Relax.......Power.......Glide"

In really tough runs, I have three challenges that occur over and over: First, I become tense when I get really tired, worried that I will struggle badly at the end. Second, I feel the loss of the bounce and strength I had at the beginning, and worry that there will be no strength later. Third, my form starts to get ragged and I worry about further deterioration of muscles and tendons and more fatigue due to "wobbling."

Over the past three decades, I have learned that it is the worry about the problems, not the problems themselves, that produces the real anxiety. I have also learned that the magic words help me stay focused on task and away from worry for a good segment of time—allowing me to run hundreds of yards down the course. The visualization of each of these positives helps a little. The real magic comes from the association I have made with hundreds of

successful experiences when I started to "lose it" in one of the three areas, but overcame the problems. Each time I "run through" one or more of the challenging situations. I associate the experience with these magic words and add to the magic.

Now, when something starts to go wrong, I repeat the three words, over and over. Instead of increasing my anxiety, the repetition of the words calms me down. Even though I don't feel as strong at mile 5 as I did at mile 1, I'm empowered just by knowing that I have a strategy and can draw upon my past experience. And, when my legs lose the efficient path and bounce, I make the adjustments that will keep me moving ahead.

When I say magic words that are associated with successful experience, there are two positive effects. The saying of the words floods the brain with positive memories. For a while, the negative messages of the left brain don't have a chance and I can often run another mile or two before they return. But the second effect bestows even more power: The words directly link you to the right brain, which works intuitively to make the same connections that allowed you solve the problems before.

To be successful on any day, you only need to finish the race. Most of the time, you can get through the "bad parts" by not giving up and simply putting one foot in front of the other. If the body has done all of the training necessary, you will have pushed beyond the negative left brain messages during a series of workouts and earlier races. This produces the confidence to do this again and again. Feel free to use my magic words, or develop your own. The more experiences you have which are associated with the words, the more magic they have.

III. Dirty tricks

The strategy of the rehearsal drill will get you focused and organized, while reducing the stress of the first few miles. Magic words will pull you along through most of the training and race challenges. But on the really rough days, it helps to have some tricks to play on the left side of the brain.

"Dirty Tricks" are quick fixes that distract the left brain for a while, allowing you to get down the road or the track for 300 yards or more. These imaginative and sometimes crazy images may not have any logic behind them. But when you counter a left brain message with a creative idea, you often confuse the left brain and stop the flow of negative messages—at least for a while.

Dirty Trick #1: The giant invisible rubber band

When I get tired on long or hard runs, I unpack this secret weapon, and throw it around someone ahead of me—or someone who had the audacity to pass me. For a while, the person doesn't realize that he or she has been "looped" and continues to push onward while I get the benefit of being pulled along. After a minute or two of mentally projecting myself into this image, I have to laugh for believing in such an absurd notion. But laughing activates the creative right side of the brain. This usually generates several more entertaining ideas, especially when you do this on a regular basis.

The right brain has millions of dirty tricks. Once you get it activated, you are likely to experience solutions to current problems. Once activated with the first "dirty trick", the right side may entertain you the rest of the way.

For many more dirty tricks and mental strategies, see **Galloway's Book on Running**, 2nd Edition and **Marathon—You Can Do It**.

Note: *Nancy Clark is my advisor in sports nutrition. She has helped thousands, and gives the reasons behind her advice. JG*

Mastering Sports Tips for Aging Runners

by Nancy Clark, MS, RD

Nutrition:

One hundred years ago, life expectancy was 42 years. Today, most of us will live twice as long. With age, we gain not only wrinkles and gray hair, but also wisdom, an appreciation for our mortality and the desire to protect our good health. As an aging runner, you also have the desire to remain energetic, if not competitive. You may wonder if you have significantly different sports nutrition needs from younger athletes. To date, the research suggests that older athletes have no hugely different nutritional needs other than to optimize your daily sports diet so you'll have every possible edge over the younger folks.

Your biggest nutrition concern should be to routinely eat quality calories from nutrient-dense, health protective foods that—
• invest in top performance,
• enhance recovery from hard workouts, and
• reduce the risk of heart disease, cancer, osteoporosis and other debilitating diseases of aging.

The following nutrition tips can help you create a winning food plan that's appropriate for all runners, including those in this marathon called life! Don't end up like Mickey Mantle who once said, "If I'd known I was going to live this long, I would have taken better care of myself..."

If you haven't already done so, shape up your diet! The diseases of aging are actually the diseases of poor nutrition (and inactivity). Eating well reduces the risk of weight gain, high blood pressure, diabetes, heart disease, colon cancer and osteoporosis. Eating well also supports your training program. Don't let nutrition be the missing link in your plan to run past 100. Meeting with a sports dietitian can help you optimize your dietary intake. To find a local sports dietitian, go to www.eatright.org and put your zip code into the "Find a Dietitian" referral network.

Carbohydrates

Focus your meals on wholesome carbs. Multi-grain bagels, rye crackers, brown rice and oatmeal are just a few examples of wholesome grain foods that both fuel muscles and protect against cancer, diabetes and heart disease. Carb-rich fruits such as bananas, orange juice, and dried fruits, as well as fruit yogurt and/or smoothies also do the job of fueling performance and protecting good health.

- Carbohydrates are not fattening; excess calories are fatting (particularly excess calories of fat). Enjoy quality carbs (grains, fruits, vegetables) as the foundation of each meal. Even dieting runners should eat carbs to fuel their muscles.

- Carbohydrates do not cause diabetes. (Lack of exercise and over-fatness are two main culprits that contribute to Type II diabetes.) Even people with diabetes can—and should—eat carbs at each meal, particularly if you are active with walking and running.

Fats

While you should limit your intake of excess calories from health-harmful foods high in saturated fat (cookies, burgers, butter, and gravy), you should increase your intake of health-promoting nuts, olive and canola oils and fish. These fats have a health-protective anti-inflammatory effect. Given that diseases of aging, such as heart disease and diabetes, are thought to be triggered by inflammation, consuming plant and fish oils that reduce inflammation is a wise choice. (For example, people who eat peanut butter five or more times per week reduce their risk of heart disease and diabetes by about 20%.)

Enjoy a little healthful fat at each meal:
- slivered almonds on granola,
- trail mix with nuts for snacks,
- salmon with dinner,
- a sprinkling of olive oil on salads.

Fat is not only satiating and abates hunger, but, in small amounts, also is an important fuel for endurance runners.

Fluids

The older you get, the less sensitive your thirst mechanism becomes. That is, you may need fluids but may not feel thirsty. Plus, older bodies have a lower water content and reduced kidney function that can also have an impact on adequate hydration. Thankfully, being fit helps counter some of the age-related changes in fluid metabolism. To reduce the risk of chronic under-hydration, drink enough so that you urinate every three to four hours. If you can last from 8 in the morning until 3 in the afternoon without having to urinate, start drinking more! Your urine should be a light color, like lemonade; not dark and concentrated. You don't have to drink plain water to satisfy your fluid needs. The water in fruit, yogurt, salads, soups and even coffee and iced tea counts toward your fluid requirement.

Weight

Even elite runners gain a little weight with age. And non-elite runners have been known to gain a lot! Staying active, in addition to eating quality calories that invest in staying healthy-- is your best weight management technique. Stay with your training program, and also stay active throughout the rest of your day. That is, taking the stairs instead of the elevator!

Calcium

Even though your bones have stopped growing, they are still alive and need to be kept strong with resistance exercise and daily calcium. This advice applies to men as well as women. By selecting a calcium-rich food at each meal (including low fat dairy or soy milk products), you'll invest in getting the Dietary Recommended Intake (DRI) of 1,200 milligrams of calcium per day. For example, runners can easily choose a nutrient-dense diet that meets their calcium needs, such as –

• Cereal with 8 ounces of milk (300 mg. calcium) for breakfast,
• 8 ounces of yogurt (400 mg. calcium) with lunch,
• a (decaf) latte (300 mg) for a snack, and
• low fat milk (300 mg) with dinner.

By choosing calcium-rich foods instead of supplements, you consume a whole package of health-protective nutrients. Calcium supplements are designed to supplement wise food choices, not replace a whole food group. You'll improve bone strength by having strong muscles attached to the bones. Be sure to do strengthening exercises such as lifting weights at least twice a week.

Vitamins

As people age, the Daily Recommended Intake for vitamins D, B-6 and B-12 increases. All vitamins have health-protective benefits, particularly vitamins E, folate, riboflavin, pyridoxine and the minerals calcium, magnesium and zinc. To insure a strong intake of these nutrients, you want to eat quality foods plus take a vitamins and mineral pill to supplement your diet for "health insurance." But also take a look at the "nutrition facts" on the food labels of to see what you are eating. For example, Powerbars and Total cereal are highly fortified with vitamins and minerals, and may already be providing more than enough to meet your needs.

While there's no harm in taking a multi-vitamin and mineral pill for health insurance, colorful fruits and vegetables are really the best all-natural sources of vitamins. By eating a rainbow of foods (blue berries, orange carrots, red tomatoes, green beans, etc.), you consume not only lots of vitamin C, potassium and folic acid for heart health and blood pressure control, but also numerous phytochemicals that are thought to be cancer protective. To boost your vitamin intake through foods, enjoy at least a generous amount of fruit at breakfast (such as a big banana on cereal + a glass of orange juice) and a pile of colorful vegetables at lunch and/or dinner (a big salad and/or a pile of steamed broccoli). Also keep exercising: the more you exercise, the more you eat—and the more vitamins you consume.

Take note: If you have switched to an "all natural" and "whole foods" diet, be aware these products are not fortified or enriched with extra vitamins. Hence, you might want to mix and match the "all natural foods" with standard foods. That is, keep eating your Wheaties along with your Kashi.

Anti-oxidant vitamins

Anti-oxidant vitamin supplements such as C and E are popular among aging athletes but the research has yet to support this practice. The body responds to extra exercise by making extra anti-oxidants. The body also responds with a larger appetite. The trick is to satisfy the bigger appetite by eating more vitamin-rich fruits and veggies rather than cookies and desserts. These wholesome foods offer compounds that work synergistically and are more powerful than vitamin pills.

Whereas adequate vitamins are good for your health, too many anti-oxidants might be bad for your health. For example, in (younger) Ironman triathletes, high doses (800 IU) of vitamin E created a harmful inflammatory effect when taken for 8 weeks before the Hawaii Ironman Triathlon. The lead researcher of the study, Dr. David Nieman, believes too many anti-oxidants can convert into pro-oxidants. This generates an undesirable imbalance that exerts pro-inflammatory effects, the opposite of what is desired. (Nieman, Med Sci Sports Exerc, August 2004). The bottom line: If you choose to take antioxidant supplements, limit your intake to the tolerable upper limit (2,000 milligrams C and 1,000 milligrams E).

As people get older, they tend to exercise less—even athletes, and that means they consume less food. An active 80-year-old man requires about 200 calories less than when he was 50; an active 80 year old woman, about 150 fewer calories. This is likely due to the fact they are exercising less, or less active throughout the entire day (taking more naps). But with fewer calories taken in, they are consuming fewer vitamins. If this sounds familiar, be sure to take your daily multi-vitamin and mineral pill. The "Senior Formula" is best, because it is geared towards the needs of older people. For example, Centrum Silver contains no iron because too much iron, in people who are not iron-deficient, may be associated with heart disease. It also contains a strong dose of E, B-6, B-12 and chromium, because these nutrients might be health-protective to older people.

Note: most multi-vitamin and mineral pills contain very little calcium because calcium takes up too much space and the pill gets too big to enjoyably swallow. That's why a separate calcium pill is important for people who fail to meet their calcium needs via their diet.

Recovery

If you are recovering slowly from workouts, take a good look at your post-run refueling practices. To stay up with the young kids (or grand kids), have a carb-protein combination within the hour after you exercise, and another one two hours later. Enjoy chocolate milk, fruit yogurt, a bowl of cereal with milk, a sandwich, or a meal. Your muscles need the protein to rebuild and heal and the carbs to refuel. The sooner you consume them, the better you'll recover!

Maintaining muscles

When it comes to maintaining strong muscles, the saying holds true: Use 'em or lose 'em! You can thwart the age-related decline in muscle mass by strength training at least twice a week. Not only do strong muscles keep you powerful, but also help keep your metabolism from slowing. That is, your metabolic rate is driven by the amount of muscle you have. The more muscle mass, the more calories you need—and the more health-protective protein, vitamins and minerals you consume.

Protein

To build, maintain and repair your muscles, you need to eat adequate protein on a daily basis. As you age, your protein needs to slightly increase—but not enough to have a separate protein recommendation. The target intake for athletes is 0.6 to 0.8 grams protein per pound body weight (1.2 to 1.7 gm pro/kg) if you are consuming adequate calories. If you are restricting calories (i.e., dieting), you need to eat a little more protein because, when you are in calorie deficit, your body burns protein for fuel instead of using it to build and repair muscles. For a 150 pound senior runner, the target protein intake is 90 to 120 grams of protein per day. To reach this target, plan to eat protein with each meal every day, in addition to the protein you get with your calcium-rich milk or yogurt.

Example:
- toast with peanut butter (10 g) + a latte (10 g)
- sandwich with 2 ounces turkey (15g) + 1 ounce low fat cheese (7g) + a yogurt (10 g)
- handful of nuts for a snack (10 g)
- spaghetti with meat sauce (25 g) + 8-oz. milk (12 g).
- Red meat, reputed to be bad for heart health, can actually be a welcome addition to a sports diet as long as it is lean. (The amount of cholesterol in beef is similar to that of chicken and fish.) Lean beef offers not only protein but also iron, zinc, B-vitamins and other nutrients important for aging athletes.
- Protein-rich fish--in particular salmon, swordfish, tuna and

other oily fish––offer health-protective fats that reduce the risk of heart disease, as well as cancer and the discomfort of rheumatoid arthritis. Because these fish may contain undesired mercury, limit your intake to twelve ounces of cooked fish per week (two to three servings).

- If you prefer a vegetarian diet, enjoy generous amounts of beans, nuts and soy. Consuming a protein-rich plant food at each meal can supply adequate protein. Enjoy chopped walnuts in oatmeal, hummus in a pita pocket, tofu in a stir-fry.

Glucosamine and Chondroitin

If you have mild to moderate osteoarthritis, you might be curious about glucosamine and chondroitin, two supplements reported to relieve pain and possibly slow cartilage damage. The National Institutes of Health have just completed in-depth research to determine the effectiveness of these supplements. The results of the study (involving 1,583 people with an average age of 59) suggest the supplements are not much better than a placebo at relieving mild knee pain, but offer some benefits to those with moderate to severe knee pain.

Some professionals are questioning the results of the study, based on the form of supplement used. Until more in-depth research offers more information, if you choose to take these alternatives to aspirin and NSAIDS:

- be sure to buy brands from a large, well-established company that may offer better quality than glucosamine or chondroitin from smaller, less expensive brands.
- take the amount used in research studies: generally 1,500 mg/day of glucosamine and 1,200 mg/day of chondroitin. This might cost $1 to $3 per day.
- stop using them if you feel no beneficial response in 6 to 8 weeks. Not everyone responds.
- abstain from chondroitin if you are taking blood-thinning medication. Chondroitin can act as a blood-thinner.

Iron

Post-menopausal women do not need extra iron, so the iron needs for men and women are similar. You should not take iron supplements because too much iron, in people who are not iron-deficient, may be associated with heart disease.

If you are taking aspirin and NSAIDS for arthritis and joint pain, be aware of the possibility of blood losses due to intestinal bleeding caused by the medications. In such case, you might find yourself anemic and in need of supplemental iron.

Drug-nutrient Interactions

Some foods interact with medications, making them less effective. For example, if you are taking a cholesterol lowering medication such as Lipitor, you should not eat grapefruit. Other medications need extra nutrition. For example, if you are taking diuretics, you should eat potassium-rich fruits (oranges, bananas) and vegetables (potatoes). Always check with your pharmacist to determine if any of your medications have special nutrition considerations.

Memory support

Blue-purple fruits, such as blueberries, purple grape juice and Concord grapes are especially rich in health protective compounds that enhance communication within the nervous system. According to James Joseph, Ph.D. from the USDA Human Nutrition Research Center at Tufts University in Boston, blue-purple fruits contribute to powerful improvements in brain activity patterns that reverse the deleterious effects of aging in rats. Joseph is optimistic his rat research will hold true with humans.

If so, eating more blueberries and drinking purple grape juice could potentially prevent the onset of symptoms of Parkinson's and Alzheimer's diseases. Hence, Joseph suggests we consume these foods more frequently:

- grape juice is carbohydrate-rich and an excellent recovery food.
- frozen blueberries are a tasty topping for breakfast cereal.
- dried blueberries are available at most whole foods stores — delicious as snacks by the handful!

Probiotics

While you may know that antibiotics are used to kill the bad bugs in your body, you may not know about probiotics. Probiotics (which means "good for life") are used to enhance the growth of good bacteria in your intestines. These bacteria do good things, like produce essential fats, enhance digestion and nutrient absorption, and bolster the immune system. (Seventy percent of immune function is based in the intestinal tract). Athletes who benefit from probiotics include those who:

1. take antibiotics (they kill both bad and good bacteria);
2. suffer from diarrhea, constipation or other bowel disorders;
3. are critically ill or have had surgery.

Yogurt and kefir are examples of probiotics. We can all benefit by using probiotics as preventive nutrition. Perhaps a yogurt a day can help keep the doctor away! To boost your probiotic intake, enjoy more yogurt (with live cultures) or other cultured milk products such as kefir or Dannon's DanActive. You could also take probiotics supplements. Three commonly used products include VSL #3, Cultural (by Danone), and Flora Q (by Bradley Pharmaceuticals).

Fiber

Eat enough fiber-rich foods to have regular bowel movements; this not only enhances sports comfort but also invests in good health. The fiber in oatmeal, for example, reduces cholesterol and risk of heart disease. Foods richest in fiber include bran cereal, bran breads, and whole grains such as brown rice and corn. Fruits and veggies are also good sources.

The bottom line

- Eat wisely—quality calories.
- Enjoy carbs as the foundation of each meal and protein as the accompaniment.
- Include a calcium-rich food three to four times a day.
- Drink plenty of fluids.
- Lift weights.
- Refuel rapidly and enjoy feeling younger.

May wholesome foods and enjoyable exercise be thy winning edge!

Sports Nutritionist Nancy Clark, MS, RD, counsels both casual exercisers and competitive athletes in her private practice at Healthworks (617-383-6100), the premier fitness center in Chestnut Hill MA. She is author of the best-selling Nancy Clark's Sports Nutrition Guidebook ($23) and her Food Guide for Marathoners: Tips for Everyday Champions ($20). Both books are available via www.nancyclarkrd.com or by sending a check to Sports Nutrition Services, PO Box 650124, West Newton MA 02465.

Balanced Diet

Complete
Multi Vitamins
and Minerals A-Z
One A Day

A-Z

Should We Take Vitamins?

The following is a contribution from Todd Whitthorne, the president and COO of Cooper Concepts, Inc., who is my advisor in the research-noted effects of vitamins and minerals. Under the direction of Dr. Kenneth Cooper and a team of consultants from four leading universities, Cooper Concepts has produced Cooper Complete, a series of nutritional products based upon years of research about how supplements can positively impact the risk factors associated with cardiovascular problems and cancer, while promoting a high level of vitality and performance. To see more about the research behind the Cooper Complete products, visit *www.CooperComplete.com* JG

As a general rule, every adult, regardless of age, would benefit from a daily multivitamin and an omega 3 (the "good" fat) supplement. From a nutrition standpoint, the body needs 6 things: fat, protein, carbohydrate, vitamins, minerals and water. Energy is derived from fat, protein and carbohydrates, but the vitamins and minerals serve primarily as catalysts for reactions within the body that help release the energy. If one develops deficiencies, then normal body functions break down. This will decrease performance and increase the risk for disease.

Since everyone is unique and ages differently, I do not have specific recommendations for folks in various decades of life. However, as we age the need for supplementation increases for a variety of reasons. One is that as we get older, we often eat less which decreases the opportunity to provide the body with the vitamins and minerals that are so important to overall health. It's also important to note that as we age, the body tends to absorb some of the B vitamins (in particular B12) from supplements better than those from food. A recent study by the Lewin Group, a research organization in Washington, D.C., indicated that the five-year estimate of potential net savings resulting from daily vitamin intake for adults over the age of 65 was $1.6 billion (9/24/2003).

A well-formulated multivitamin and Omega 3 supplement will also help reduce inflammation which is associated with a number of health conditions including cardiovascular disease, diabetes, stroke, etc. Excessive training can also increase inflammation by increasing oxidation. The original formulation of Cooper Complete has been clinically shown to lower inflammation, as measured by C-reactive protein, by 32% (*American Journal of Medicine*, December 2003). I would recommend our Elite Athlete multivitamin and mineral formulation for anyone, regardless of age, who is running over 30 miles per week.

Remember that a multivitamin is not a replacement for a bad diet; it's a "supplement." Start with a good balanced diet that includes lean protein and plenty of fruits and vegetables and think of the multivitamin as insurance. Also, do not overlook the incredible benefits of Omega 3 fatty acids. These are the "good" fats that are

"essential" which means our bodies can't make them, and we have to consume them. Not only are the Omega 3s terrific for the heart (they lower resting heart rate, blood pressure, triglycerides, risk of arrhythmia, etc.), but they also are great for the brain.

Remember our brain is only about 2-3% of our body weight but it consumes about 20-30% of our calories, 20% of our blood and 20% of our oxygen. The brain is about 60% fat, so increasing our consumption of the healthy fats (Omega 3s) is literally "essential." We know that two outstanding ways to lower the risk of depression is to be physically active and to get plenty of Omega 3s in the diet. The best source of omega 3s is either fish (ideally fatty fish like salmon) or fish oil supplements. If you take a fish oil supplement, make sure you get at least 1,000 milligrams of EPA and DHA per day. EPA (eicosapentanoic acid) and DHA (docosahexanoic acid) are the "long chain" Omega 3s that are the most beneficial. Omega 3s from plant sources (i.e. flax, walnuts, canola oil) are shorter chain omega 3s and not nearly as beneficial as EPA and DHA. The Cooper Complete Advanced Omega 3 product is a 60% concentration of EPA/DHA rather than the usual 30% concentration you find in most fish oil products. To reduce the incidence of "burp back" keep your fish oil in the refrigerator and be sure to take with meals.

Note: For more information on vitamin research, specific vitamins by age, and special needs, see *www.Cooper Complete.com* JG

Why Does Your Body Want to Hold Onto Fat?

Fat is our biological insurance policy against disaster. It is the fuel your body can use, in case of starvation, sickness, injury to the digestive system, etc. You'll read a bit later about how your biological "set point" programs your body to hold onto fat at any age. Running is one of the few ways that folks over 50 can at least keep the fat level from rising, and may help in reducing. I've spent years looking into this topic, and talking to experts in the field. This chapter will explain my beliefs about the process so that you can set up a strategy, based upon your needs and goals, and take control over a major part of this process.

Many people start running to burn fat. Indeed, the run-walk method is probably the most effective and convenient exercise mode for re-organizing your fat storage to burn fat. This method has helped thousands learn to enjoy endurance exercise—which acts like a fat-burning furnace. When the body is conditioned for fat burning, it prefers this as fuel, because of the small amount of waste product produced.

But it's not enough to burn the fat. For long term health and body management, you need to keep it off. Successful fat burners do three things:
1. Understand the process by reading this chapter and other sources.
2. Truly believe that they can maintain or lower the body fat percentage.
3. Set up a behavioral plan that fits into their lifestyle.

How does fat accumulate?

When you eat some fat during a snack or a meal, you might as well put it into a syringe and inject it into your stomach or thigh. A gram of fat eaten is a gram of fat deposited in the fat storage areas on your body. In addition, when you eat more calories than you burn during a day from protein (fish, chicken, beef, tofu) and carbohydrate (breads, fruits, vegetables, sugar), the excess is converted into fat and stored.

Fat for survival

More than a million years of evolution have programmed the human body to hold on to the fat you have stored due to a powerful principle: the survival of the species. Before humans understood disease and prevention, they were susceptible to sweeping infections. Even mild diseases and flu wiped out a significant percentage of the population, regularly, in primitive times. Those who had adequate fat stores survived periods of starvation and sickness, produced children, and passed on the fat accumulation adaptation.

The powerful Set Point holds onto our fat

The set point is a biologically engineered survival mechanism. While it does seem possible to adjust it, you are going into battle against survival mechanisms that have been in place for over a million years. The tools in this chapter can help you understand the process and take command over your own fat-burning.

Fat level is set in early 20s

Many experts agree that by about the age of 25 we have accumulated a level of fat that the body intuitively marks as its lowest level. This "set point" is programmed to increase a little each year. Let's say that John had 10% body fat at age 25, and his set point increased by half a percent per year. The amount of increase is so small when we are young, that we usually don't realize that it is happening—until about 10 years later, when it's time to go to a class reunion.

We humans are supposed to carry around fat. But your set point does too good a job, continuing to add to the percentage, each year, every year. And the amount of increase seems to be significantly greater as we get older. Unfortunately, the set point has a good memory. When you've had a tough year due to stress or illness and didn't add the usual increase, the set point over-compensates by increasing appetite during the following year or two. Go ahead; shout "Unfair!" as loud as you wish. Your set point doesn't argue— it just makes another deposit. But there's hope through exercise.

Men and women deposit fat differently

While men tend to deposit fat on the surface of the skin, women (particularly in their 20s and 30s) fill up internal storage areas first. Most women will acknowledge that their weight is rising slightly, year by year, but aren't concerned because there is no noticeable fat increase on the outside. The "pinch test" is how many people monitor their fat increase.

When the internal storage areas fill up, extra fat starts accumulating on the stomach, thighs and other areas. A common woman's complaint in the 30s or early 40s is the following: "My body has betrayed me." In fact, fat has often been deposited at a fairly consistent rate but hidden from view for many years.

Men usually find it easier to burn fat than women

When men start running regularly, many lose fat and weight for several months. Probably related to biological issues, and primitive protections for mothers, women have a harder time losing fat. The reality is that you are ahead of the others in our society....even if you are maintaining the same weight. Because of the set point, one would expect an average 45 year old person in the US to gain 3-4 pounds a year. So maintaining weight and holding the set point steady is a huge fat management victory.

Diets don't work because of the "starvation reflex"

We are certainly capable lowering food intake for days, weeks and months to lower fat levels and weight. This is a form of starvation and the set point has a long-term memory. Many folks diet and lose 10 pounds during the 2 months before the class reunion. Then, when the diet ends, the starvation rebound occurs: a slight increase in appetite and hunger occurs, over weeks and months, until the fat percentage accumulated on your body is higher that it was before the diet. It's a fact that almost all of those who lose fat on a diet put more pounds back on the body within months of going off the diet.

The starvation reflex: Waiting too long to eat triggers it

When you wait more than 3 hours without eating something, your set point organism senses that you may be going into a period of starvation. The longer you wait to eat, the more you will feel these three effects of the starvation reflex:

1. *A reduction in your metabolism rate.* Imagine an internal voice saying something like this "if this person is going to start depriving me of food, I had better tune down the metabolism rate to conserve resources." A slower metabolism makes you feel more lethargic, drowsy, and unmotivated to exercise or move around. In fact, most respond by staying in their chair or the couch, minimizing motion and calorie burning.

2. *An increase in the fat-depositing enzymes.* The longer you wait to eat something, the more enzymes are produced. The next time you eat, a greater percentage of the meal will be deposited on your body.

3. *Your appetite increases.* The longer you wait to eat, the more likely it is that, for the next few meals, you will have an insatiable appetite: After a normal meal, you're still hungry.

Suddenly depriving yourself of decadent foods

I used to like a particular type of ice cream so much that I ate a quart or more of it, several nights a week. It was the reward I gave myself for reaching my exercise goals for that day. Then, on a fateful New Year's day, my wife Barb and I decided to eliminate the chocolate chip mint ice cream from our diet—after more than 10 years of enjoyment. We were successful for 2 years. A leftover box after a birthday party got us re-started on the habit, and we even increased our intake over what it had been before—due to having deprived ourselves.

You can "starve" yourself of a food that you dearly love for an extended period of time. But at some time in the future, when the food is around and no one else is.....you will tend to over-consume that food. My correction for this problem was the following:

1. I made a contract with myself: I could have a little of it whenever I wanted—while promising to be "reasonable."
2. I set a goal of enjoying one bowl a week, 5 years from now.
3. Four years from now, enjoying a bowl every 5 days
4. Three years from now, a bowl every 4 days
5. Learning to enjoy healthy sweet things, like fruit salads, energy bars, etc.

It worked! I hardly ever eat any ice cream...but sometimes enjoy a bowl if I want. This is purely for medicinal reasons, you understand.

The low-carbohydrate scam

There is no doubt that low-carb diets can help you lose weight....water weight. Such a loss is superficial and easily gained back. Here's how it works. To perform physical exertion, you need a quick energy source (for the first 15 minutes) called glycogen, which comes from eating carbohydrates, and must be replenished every day. The storage areas for glycogen are limited and glycogen is also the primary source for vital organs like the brain. About four times the amount of water is stored near the glycogen storage areas, because it is needed when glycogen is processed into energy.

By starving themselves of carbohydrates, low-carb dieters experience a severe reduction in glycogen stores. But if the glycogen isn't there, water storage is also reduced. The elimination of these two substances can produce a significant weight loss within days—continuing for a few weeks.

Fat is not being burned off. In fact, fat consumption is encouraged in many of the low-carb diets. As low carb dieters eat more fat, they often increase the fat on the body, while the water/glycogen loss will show a weight loss, due to the superficial loss of water. When water and glycogen are replaced later, the weight goes back on. Soon the overall body weight is greater than before because of the extra fat gained during the low-carb diet.

Because the glycogen energy source is low or depleted, low carbers will have little energy for exercise. This is why you will hear folks on this diet complain about how tired they are, with no desire to exercise. When they try to run, they can't finish a workout, and usually experience lack of mental focus (low glycogen means less fuel for the brain).

Even if you "tough it out" or cheat on the diet a little, your capacity to do even moderately strenuous exertions will be greatly reduced. With your energy stores near empty, exercising becomes a real struggle, and no fun.

Low-carb diet literature doesn't tell you this....

- You don't burn fat—many gain fat.
- The weight loss is usually water loss, with glycogen loss.
- Almost everyone on this diet resumes regular eating, within a few weeks or months.
- Almost all low-carb dieters gain back more weight than they lost.
- You lose the energy and motivation to exercise.
- You lose exercise capacity that can help to keep the weight off when you resume eating normally.
- Your metabolism rate goes down, making it harder to keep the weight off.

This is a type of starvation diet. I've heard from countless low-carb victims who admit that while they were on the diet, their psychological deprivation of carbs produced a significant rebound effect when they began eating them again. The cravings for bread, pastries, French fries, soft drinks, and other pound-adding foods, increased for months. The weight goes back on, and on, and on.

Like so many diets, the low-carb diet reduces the metabolism rate. This reduces the number of calories you burn per day. When you return to eating a regular diet you will not have a "metabolism furnace" to burn up the increased calories.

Lowering the set point

Your body has a wonderful ability to adapt to the regular activities that you do. It also tries to avoid stress. In the next chapter, we will talk about how to condition your muscles to be fat burning furnaces. Once you get them into shape to do this, you can move into a fat burning lifestyle. Lowering the set point is more complex, but possible, when you are regularly putting certain types of stress on your system.

Endurance running: a positive stress which can stimulate adaptations in two areas

Running regularly and long enough to produce these stresses will trigger a search for ways of reducing the stress.
* body temperature increase
* pounding or bouncing

The temperature increase from running helps you to reduce the set point

Everyone knows that when you run, you get warm or hot. The work required to lift your body off the ground raises your core body temperature. While this is usually not a health risk, if you sustain this artificial fever, at least every other day for more than about 45 minutes, you're putting a heat stress on the system. Since body fat acts like a blanket in maintaining body temperature, the body's intuitive, long term solution, is to reduce the size of this fat blanket, which then reduces the heat buildup.

The more regular you are with run-walks that build up to more than 45 minutes, the more likely it is that your set point will be reduced to avoid this repeated stress. It also helps even more to have one run-walk every week that goes beyond 90 minutes.

Bouncing and pounding

The more weight you carry, the more you will feel the pounding effect of running. If you run as often as every other day, your body senses this regular stress and searches for ways of reducing it. It will tend to adapt by reducing the extra fat baggage, reducing the bounce stress.

Cross training for fat burning

To maintain a regular dose of set-point lowering stress while minimizing orthopedic stress, cross training can help. The best activities are those that raise core body temperature, use a lot of muscle cells, and can be continued comfortably for more than 45 minutes. Cross training is done on days when you don't run. Swimming is not a good fat-burning exercise. The water absorbs temperature buildup, and therefore core body temperature doesn't rise significantly.

Good fat burning exercises
- Nordic track
- Walking
- Elliptical
- Rowing
- Exercise cycle

How to Burn More Fat?

"By running and walking for 90 minutes during one session each week, the leg muscles become fat burners. Over time, this means that you will burn more fat when you are sitting around all day at your desk and even burn it when you are sleeping at night."

Slow, aerobic running is one of the very best ways to burn fat. But most runners, during their first year, usually hold their own, showing no weight loss. This is actually a victory over the set point. First, you are avoiding the average set point inspired increase of 1-4 pounds a year. But runners are actually burning fat by maintaining weight. How can this be? Read on.

As you run, you increase the storage of glycogen and water, all over the body, to process energy and cool you down. Your blood volume also increases. All of these internal changes help you exercise better, but they cause a weight gain (not a fat gain). If your weight is the same, a year after starting endurance exercise, you have burned off several pounds of fat. Don't let the scales drive you crazy.

Long term fat burn off requires discipline and focus. If you will take responsibility for managing your eating and doing the running and walking needed, you will succeed. One secret to fat burning success is being more active all day long. Once you learn to walk instead of sit, you will be amazed at how many steps you can take per day:

Steps = Calories burned

Aerobic running burns fat
By taking liberal walk breaks, and running totally within your physical capacity (no huffing and puffing), your muscles are being supplied with enough oxygen to do the work. You are aerobic. If you run too hard, you overwhelm the capacity of the muscles, and the blood system cannot deliver enough oxygen to the muscles. You are anaerobic. Slow running burns fat, and fast running burns sugar (glycogen).

Oxygen is needed to burn fat. Therefore running at an easy pace will keep you in the aerobic, or "fat burning" zone. When you run too fast for that day, and your muscles can't get enough oxygen, you will huff and puff. This is the sign that you are building up an oxygen deficiency. Without oxygen, the muscles turn to stored glycogen, which produces a high amount of waste product.

Fat burning training program
- One slow long run-walk a week of 60 min + (90 min + is better)
- Two other slow run-walks of 45 min +
- Two-three cross training sessions of 45 min +
- Taking an additional 6-10,000 (or more) steps a day in your daily activities

Sugar-burning during the first 15 minutes of exercise

Glycogen is the quick access fuel your body uses during the first quarter hour of exercise. Those who don't exercise longer than 15 minutes will not get into fat burning, and won't train their muscles to burn this fuel. But if you have been depriving yourself of carbohydrates, as when on a low-carb diet, you'll have trouble with energy and motivation because the first 15 minutes are really tough.

When glycogen is used for fuel, it produces a significant waste product—mostly lactic acid. If you move slowly, with mostly walking, there is no significant buildup. Even when the pace feels slow, if you are huffing and puffing within the first 10 minutes, you have been going too fast (for you, on that day). When in doubt, extend your walking at the beginning and go slower.

From 15 minutes to 45 minutes you will transition into fat burning. If you are exercising within your capabilities, your body starts to break down body fat and use it as fuel. Fat is actually a more efficient fuel, producing less of a waste product. This transition continues for the next 30 minutes. By the time you've been exercising within your capabilities for 45-50 minutes, you will be burning mostly fat—if the muscles are trained to do this. With lots of walking, and a slow pace, almost anyone can work up to three sessions of 45 minutes each.

Three sessions a week, in the fat burn zone

Even the most untrained muscles that have only burned glycogen for 50 years can be trained to burn fat under two conditions:

- Exercise easily, and get into the fat-burning zone (45+ min a week).
- Do this regularly: 3 times a week (best to have no more than two days between sessions).

One session a week beyond 90 minutes

The longer session should gradually increase up to an hour and half, keeping you in the fat burn zone long enough to encourage your muscles to adapt to fat burning. For best results, this should be done every week. If you don't have time for a 90 minute session, shoot for at least 60 minutes.

Walk breaks allow you to go farther without getting tired

This pushes you into the fat burn zone while allowing for a quick recovery of the muscles. For fat-burning purposes, it is best to walk earlier and more often. The number of calories you burn is based upon the number of miles covered. Walk breaks allow you to cover more distance each day, without tiring yourself. By lowering the exertion level, you will stay in the fat burning zone longer, usually for the whole session. When in doubt, it's best to walk more and slow down.

Be realistic with yourself. Are you willing to make the lifestyle changes you'll need to burn significant fat? If you're not sure, use some of the suggestions in this chapter and look at the big picture. Even if you don't lose a pound, running regularly will give you a series of health benefits. Studies at the Cooper Clinic, founded by Dr. Kenneth Cooper in Dallas, Texas, and other organizations, have shown that even obese people lower their risk factors for heart disease when they exercise regularly. They are often much healthier than thin people who don't exercise.

How much walking and how much running?

The bottom line in fat burning is the number of calories covered per week. So, it helps to insert more walk breaks in order to cover more miles without increasing fatigue. Follow the guidelines in the Galloway Run-Walk-Run Method chapter. When in doubt, walk more. It is also better to choose a ratio that seems too easy for you—so you'll recover fast.

10,000 walking steps a day on non-running days/6,000 on running days

Adding walking steps to your day may burn more fat off your body than running. While running sets up the fat-burning process, it may trigger an appetite increase. Walking doesn't increase appetite significantly. A pedometer, or step counter, will provide an incentive to walk more. It may also provide reinforcement for adding extra steps to your day. No other device that I know will give you a sense of control over your actual calorie burn-off. Once you get into the goal of taking more than 10,000 steps a day in your everyday activities, you'll find yourself getting out of your chair more often, parking farther away from the supermarket, walking around the kid's playground, etc.

Step counters are usually about one inch square, and clip onto your belt, pocket or waistband. The simple models just count steps, which is all you need. Other models compute miles and calories. I recommend getting one from a quality manufacturer. When tested, some of the lower quality models registered 3-4 times as many steps as the quality products did—walking exactly the same course. For recommendations on step counters, see my website: *www.JeffGalloway.com*.

Your goal is to accumulate at least 10,000 walking steps at home, at work, going shopping, and waiting for grandkids, etc., on your non-running days (6,000 on your running days). This is very doable.

You will find many pockets of time during the day when you are just sitting or standing. As you increase the step count, you become a more active person and feel more energized.

About dinnertime, do a "step check." If you haven't acquired your 10,000 (or 6,000), walk around the block a few extra times before or after the meal. You don't have to stop with these figures. As you get into it, you'll find many more opportunities to walk....and burn.

Up to 59 pounds of fat....gone in one year

The fat wars are won by many small burning skirmishes—a little here, and a little there. Most of us have many opportunities. I've heard from many runners who took advantage of many of the following loopholes, every day, and burned off a dozen or more pounds in a year.

Pounds burned per year/Activity

1-2 pounds—taking the stairs instead of the elevator

10-30 pounds—getting out of your chair at work to walk down the hall

1-2 pounds—getting off the couch to move around the house (but not to get potato chips)

1-2 pounds—parking farther away from the supermarket, mall, etc

1-3 pounds—parking farther away from your work

2-4 pounds—walking around the kid's playground, practice field, doctor's office

2-4 pounds—walking up and down the concourse as you wait for your next flight

3-9 pounds—walking the dog each day

2-4 pounds—walking a couple of times around the block after supper

2-4 pounds—walking a couple of times around the block during lunch hour at work

2-4 pounds—walking an extra loop around the mall, supermarket, etc., to look for bargains

(This last one could be expensive when at the mall)

Total: 27-59 pounds a year

15 more pounds burned each year from adding a few extra miles every week

By using time periods when you usually have small pockets of time, you can add to your fat-burning without feeling extra fatigue:

- Slow down and add one more mile on each run.
- Walk a mile at lunchtime.
- Walk or jog a mile before or after dinner.

Controlling the Income Side of the Fat Equation

As you get older, your metabolism tends to slow down. Exercise (especially running and walking), will help you "rev-it-up." But gaining control over your calorie intake is crucial for body fat reduction. Runners often complain that even though they have increased mileage and faithfully done their cross-training workouts, they are not losing weight. In every case, when I have questioned them, each did not have a handle on the number of calories they were eating. In every case, when they went through the drill of quantifying, each was eating more than they thought. Below you will find ways to cut 10 or more pounds out of your diet—without starving yourself.

Websites tell you calorie balance and nutrient balance

The best tool I've found for managing your food intake is a good website or software program. There are a number of these that will help to balance your calories (calories burned vs. calories eaten). Most of these will have you log in your exercise for the day, and what you eat. At the end of the day, you can retrieve an accounting of calories, and of nutrients. If you are low on certain vitamins or minerals, protein, etc., after dinner, you can eat food or take a vitamin pill.

- Use a website that accounts for age. Your intake will be compared with what is needed—for you.
- Some programs will tell vegetarians whether they have received enough complete protein, since this nutrient is harder to put together from vegetable sources.
- If you haven't received enough of some nutrient, you can do something about it the next day to make up the deficit.
- If you ate too many calories, walk after dinner, boost tomorrow's workouts, reduce the calories, or do all of the above.

I don't recommend letting any web site control your life. At first, it helps to use it every day for 1-2 weeks. During this time, you'll see patterns, and note where you tend to need supplementation or should cut back. After this initial period, do a spot check for 2-3 days. Some folks need more spot checks than others. If you are more motivated to eat the right foods and quantities by logging in every day, go for it.

For a list of the websites, see my website: *www.jeffgalloway.com*. Try several out before you decide.

Learning portion control—the greatest benefit

Whether you use a web site or not, a very productive drill is that of logging what you eat every day for a week. Bring a little note pad, and a small scale if you need it. As people record and then analyze the calories in each portion, they are usually surprised at the number of calories (and fat grams) they are eating. Many foods have fat and simple sugars so well disguised that you don't realize how quickly the calories add up.

After doing this drill for several days you have a tool that can help you adjust the size of your portions. This is a major step in taking control over the income side of the fat equation. Many runners have told me that they resented the first week of logging in, but it became fairly routine after that. Once you get used to doing this, you become aware of what you will be putting in your mouth, and can take make better food choices. Now, you're gaining control over your eating behaviors.

Eating every 2 hours

As mentioned in the previous chapter, if you have not eaten for about 3 hours, your body senses that it is going into a starvation mode and slows down the metabolism rate while increasing the production of fat-depositing enzymes. This means that you will not be burning as many calories as normal, and you won't tend to be as mentally and physically alert. Because of this, more of your next meal will be stored away as fat.

You can often burn more fat by eating more often. If the starvation reflex starts working after 3 hours, then you can beat it by eating every 2 hours. A person who now eats 2-3 times a day, can burn 8-10 more pounds a year when they shift to eating 8-10 times a day. This assumes that the same calories are eaten using each eating pattern.

Big meals slow you down

Big meals are a big production for the digestive system. Blood is diverted to the long and winding intestine and the stomach. Because of the workload, the body tends to shut down blood flow to other areas, leaving you feeling more lethargic and sedentary.

Small meals speed you up

Smaller amounts of food can usually be processed quickly without putting a burden on the digestive system. Each time you eat a small meal or snack, your metabolism speeds up. By revving up the metabolism, several times a day, you will burn more calories.

You also give a setback to your set point

When you wait more than three hours between meals, the set point engages the starvation reflex. But if you eat every 2-3 hours, the set point is not engaged—due to the regular supply of food. Therefore the fat depositing enzymes don't have to be stimulated.

No more tiredness?

Motivation increases when we eat more often. The most common reason I've found for low motivation in the afternoon is not eating regularly enough during the day—especially during the afternoon. If you have not eaten for 4 hours or more, and you're scheduled for a run that afternoon, you will not feel very motivated because of low blood sugar and low metabolism. Even when you've had a bad eating day, and feel down in the dumps, you can gear up for a run-walk by having a snack 30-60 minutes before exercise. A fibrous energy bar with a cup of coffee (tea, diet drink) can reverse the negative mindset. But you don't have to get yourself into this situation if you eat solid snacks every 2-3 hours.

Satisfaction from a small meal will reduce overeating

The number of calories you eat each day can be reduced by choosing foods (and nutrient combinations) that leave you satisfied longer. Sugar is the worst problem in calorie control and satisfaction. When you drink a beverage with sugar in it, the sugar will be processed very quickly, and you will often be hungry within 30 minutes—even after consuming a high quantity of calories. This will usually lead to two undesirable outcomes:

1. Eating more food to satisfy hunger (calories not needed are processed into fat)
2. Staying hungry and triggering the starvation reflex

Your mission is to find the right combination of foods in your small meals that will leave you satisfied for 2-3 hours. Then, eat another

snack that will do the same. You can find a growing number of food combinations that have fewer calories, but keep you from getting hungry until your next snack.

Nutrients that leave you satisfied longer:

Fat

Even a little fat, added to a snack, can leave you more satisfied because it slows down digestion. Caution: a little goes a long way. When the fat content of a meal goes beyond 30%, you start to feel more lethargic because fat is harder to digest. While up to about 18% of the calories in fat will help you hold hunger at bay, a lot of fat can compromise a fat-burning program. Fat is automatically deposited on your body. None of the dietary fat is used for energy. When you eat a fatty meal, you might as well inject it onto your hips or stomach. The fat you burn as fuel must be broken down from the stored fat on your body. Conclusion: It helps to eat a little fat with a snack, but a lot of it will mean more fat on your body.

There are two kinds of fat that have been found to cause narrowing of the arteries around the heart and leading to your brain: saturated fat and Trans fat. Mono and unsaturated fats from vegetable sources are often healthy—olive oil, nuts, avocado, safflower oil. Some fish oils have Omega 3 fatty acids which have been shown to have a protective effect on the heart. Many fish, however, have oil that is not protective.

Look carefully at the labels. Many foods have vegetable oils that have been processed into Trans fat. A wide range of baked goods and other foods have this negative component. If you have questions, call the 800 number on food packages that don't break down the fat composition—or avoid the food.

Protein—Lean protein is best

This nutrient is needed, every day, for the rebuilding of muscle that is broken down during exercise, as well as normal wear and tear. Runners, even those who log high mileage, don't need to eat significantly more protein than sedentary people. But if runners don't get their usual amount of protein, they feel more aches and pains along with a sense of overall weakness, sooner than sedentary people.

Having protein with each meal will leave you feeling satisfied for a longer period of time. But eating unnecessary protein calories will produce a conversion of the excess into fat.

Recently, protein has been added to sports drinks with great success. When a drink with 80% carbohydrate and 20% protein (such as Accelerade) is consumed within 30 minutes before the start of a run, glycogen is better activated and energy is supplied sooner. By consuming a drink that has the same ratio (like Endurox R4) within 30 minutes after finishing a run, you'll reload the muscles better and more quickly.

Water

As you can see in Nancy Clark's chapter in this book, thirst is not a good indicator of dehydration, as we get older. It is best to drink about 8 oz of water about every 2 hours. The "8 glasses a day" of fluid recommendation is a good quota to shoot for—unless your doctor recommends more. You will only get half of the fluid in caffeinated beverages. Alcohol causes dehydration. It's best to minimize alcohol consumption and to add a glass of water to your quota, for each beer or glass of wine consumed.

Complex carbohydrates

These carbs give you a "discount" and a "grace period."
Foods such as celery, beans, cabbage, spinach, turnip greens, grape nuts, whole grain cereal, etc., can burn up to 25 % of the calories in digestion. As opposed to fat (which is directly deposited on your body after eating it), it is only the excess carbs that are processed

into fat. After dinner, for example, you have the opportunity to burn off any excess that you acquired during the day by walking around the neighborhood or getting on the treadmill.

Fat + Protein + Complex Carbs = SATISFACTION

Eating a snack that has a variety of the three satisfaction ingredients above will lengthen the time that you'll feel satisfied—even after small meals. These three items take longer to digest, reduce the temptation to eat more calories and "rev up" the metabolism rate.

Fiber

A greater amount of fiber in foods will slow down digestion and sustain a longer feeling of satisfaction. Soluble fiber, such as oat bran, seems to bestow a longer feeling of satisfaction than insoluble fiber such as wheat bran. But any type of fiber will help in this regard.

Recommended percentages of the three nutrients:

There are differing opinions on this issue. Here are the ranges given by a number of top nutritionists that I have read and asked. These are listed in terms of the percentage per day of each of the calories consumed in each nutrient, compared to the total number of calories consumed per day.

Protein: between	*18% and 28%*
Fat: between	*15% and 25%*
Carbohydrate:	*whatever is left*
	—hopefully in complex carbohydrates.

Simple carbs help us put weight back on the body

Fact: We're going to eat some simple carbohydrates. These are the "feel good" foods, such as candy, baked sweets, starches (mashed potatoes and rice), sugar drinks (including fruit juice and sports drinks) and most desserts. When you are on a fat burning mission you need to minimize the amount of these foods that you eat.

The sugar in these products is digested so quickly that you get little or no lasting satisfaction from them. They often leave you with a craving for more of them, which, if denied, will produce a starvation reflex. Because they are processed quickly, you become hungry more quickly and will want to eat. This results in accumulating extra calories that usually end up as fat at the end of the day.

As mentioned in the last chapter, it is never a good idea to totally eliminate them by saying something like "I'll never eat another." This sets up a starvation reflex ticking time bomb. Keep taking a bite or two of the foods you dearly love, while cultivating the taste of foods with more fiber and little or no refined sugar or starch.

Good Blood Sugar = Motivation

"Mature runners often need to manage their blood sugar more than they did in younger days."

The blood sugar level (BSL) determines how good you feel. When it is stable, you feel energized and motivated. If you eat too much sugar, your BSL can rise too high. You'll feel really good for a while, but the excess sugar triggers a release of insulin, that usually pushes it too low. In this state, you don't have energy, mental focus is foggy and motivation drops rapidly.

When blood sugar level is maintained throughout the day, you will be more motivated to exercise, and feel like adding other movement to your life. Overall, you'll have a more positive mental attitude and will be able to deal with stress and solve problems. Just as eating throughout the day keeps metabolism up, the steady infusion of balanced nutrients all day long will maintain stable blood sugar.

You don't want to get on the "bad side" of your BSL. Low levels are a stress on the system and literally mess with your mind. Your brain is fueled by blood sugar and when the supply goes down, your mental stress goes up. If you have not eaten for several hours before a run-walk, you'll receive an increase in the number of negative messages that say that you don't have the energy to exercise or that it will hurt.

The simple act of eating a snack that has carbohydrate and about 20% protein will reduce the negative, make you feel good and get you out the door. Keeping a snack as a BSL booster can often be the difference whether you run that day or not.

The BSL roller coaster

Eating a snack with too many calories of simple carbohydrate can be counter productive for BSL maintenance. As mentioned above, when the sugar level gets too high, your body produces insulin, sending BSL lower than before. The tendency is to eat again, which produces excess calories that are converted into fat. But if you don't eat, you'll stay hungry and miserable and will be in no mood to exercise or move around and burn calories (or get in your run for the day).

Eating every 2-3 hours is best

Once you find which snacks work best to maintain your BSL, most people maintain a stable blood sugar level better by eating small meals regularly, every 2-3 hours. As noted in the previous chapter, it's best to combine complex carbs with protein and a small amount of fat.

Eat before running if blood sugar is low

Most that run-walk in the morning don't need to eat anything before they start. As mentioned above, if your blood sugar level is low in the afternoon, and you have a run scheduled, a snack can help when taken about 30 minutes before the run. If you feel that a morning snack will help, the only issue is to avoid consuming so much that you get an upset stomach.

For best results in raising blood sugar when it is too low (within 30 minutes before a run), a snack should have about 80% of the calories in simple carbohydrate and 20% in protein. This promotes the production of insulin, which is helpful before a run in getting the glycogen in your muscles ready for action. The product Accelerade has worked best among the thousands of runners I hear from every year. It has the 80/20 ratio of carb to protein. If you eat an energy bar with the 80/20 ratio, be sure to drink 6-8 oz of water.

Eating during exercise

Most exercisers don't need to eat or drink during a run-walk until the length of the session exceeds 90 minutes. At this point, there are several options. If you are prone to low blood sugar problems, you may want to start taking your snacks within the first 20 minutes. Most runners wait until about 40 minutes before starting.

GU or Gel products: These come in small packets, and are the consistency of honey or thick syrup. The most successful way to take them is to put 1-2 packets in a small plastic bottle with a pop-top. About every 10-15 minutes, take 2-3 small squirts with a sip or two of water.

Energy bars: Cut into 8-10 pieces and take a piece, with a couple of sips of water, every 10-15 minutes.

Candy: Stick particularly to Gummi bears or hard candies. The usual consumption is 1-2 about every 10 minutes.

Sports drinks: Since there is a significant percentage of runners who experience nausea when they drink this type of product during exercise, I don't recommend it during a run. If you have found this to work for you, use it exactly as you have used it before.

It is important to re-load after exercise—within 30 minutes

Whenever you have finished a hard or long workout (for you), a reloading snack will help you recover faster. Again, the 80/20 ratio of carb to protein has been most successful in reloading the muscles. The product that has worked best among the thousands I work with each year is Endurox R4.

Cross Training: Getting Better as You Rest the Legs

Older runners can benefit more from cross training than younger runners. By taking more days off from running, the amount and/or the intensity of each running day can increase. When the right cross training is done on the "running rest days," it's possible to improve strength, run more efficiently and burn more fat while allowing the calf muscles to rebound for the next run.

Cross training activities

Cross training simply means "alternative exercise" to running. Your goal is to find exercises that give you a good feeling of exertion, but do not fatigue the workhorses of running: calf muscles, achilles tendon and feet. Since the various activities bestow different benefits, you can select your cross training program to produce the effects you wish.

The other exercises don't deliver the same post-run afterglow as a run. Many runners report that it may take a combination of 3 or 4 segments in a session to feel like they've had a real workout. But even if you don't get the same running-endorphin boost, you'll receive the relaxation that comes from exercise, while you burn calories and fat.

When you start any exercise (or are starting back, after a layoff):

1. Start with 5 easy minutes of exercise, rest for 20 or more minutes and do 5 more easy minutes.
2. Take a day of rest between this exercise (you can do a different exercise the next day).
3. Increase by 2-3 additional minutes each session until you get to the number of minutes that gives you the appropriate feeling of exertion.
4. Once you have reached two 15 minute sessions, you could shift to one 22-25 minute session and increase by 2-3 more minutes per session if you wish
5. It's best to do no exercise the day before a long run, a very hard speed session or a race.
6. To maintain your conditioning in each alternative exercise, do one session each week of 10 minutes or more once you reach that amount. If you have the time, you can cross-train (XT) on all of your days off from running—except listed in #5 above.
7. The maximum amount of cross training is up to the individual. As long as you are feeling fine for the rest of the day and having no trouble with your runs the next day, the length of your cross training should not be a problem.

Water running can improve your running form

All of us have little flips and side motions of our legs that reduce our running efficiency. During a water running workout, the resistance of the water forces your legs to find a more efficient path. In addition, several leg muscles are strengthened which can help to keep your legs on a smoother path when they get tired at the end of a long run.

Here's how!

You'll need a flotation belt for this exercise. The product "aqua jogger" is designed to float you off the bottom of the pool. Pull in the elastic belt so that it is close to the body. There are many other ways to keep you floating, including water ski float belts and life jackets.

Get in the deep end of the pool and move your legs through a running motion. This means little or no knee lift, kicking out slightly in front of you, and bringing the leg behind, with the foot coming up behind you. As in running, your lower leg should be parallel with the horizontal during the back-kick.

If you are not feeling much exertion, you're probably lifting the knees too high and moving your legs through a small range of motion. To get the benefit, an extended running motion is needed.

It's important to do water running once a week to keep the adaptations that you have gained. If you miss a week, you should drop back a few minutes from your previous session. If you miss more than 3 weeks, start back at two 5-8 min sessions.

Fat burning and overall fitness exercises

Nordic track

This exercise machine simulates the motion used in cross country skiing. It is one of the best cross training modes for fat burning because it allows you to use a large number of muscle cells while raising body temperature. If you exercise at an easy pace, you can get into the fat burning zone (past 45 minutes) after a gradual buildup to that amount. This exercise requires no pounding of the legs or feet, and should allow you to run as usual the next day.

Rowing machine

There are a number of different types of rowing machines. Some work the legs a bit too hard for a recovery day workout, but most allow you to use a wide variety of lower and upper body muscle groups. Like Nordic track, if you have the right machine for you, it's possible to continue to exercise for about as long as you wish, once you have gradually worked up to this. Most of the better machines are good fat-burners; they use a large number of muscle cells, raise temperature, and can be continued for more than three-quarters of an hour.

Cycling

Indoor cycling (on an exercise cycle) is a better fat burner exercise than outdoor cycling, because it raises your body temperature more. You don't get the cooling effect of the breeze that you generate on a real bike. The muscles used in both indoor and outdoor cycling are mostly the quadriceps—on the front of the thigh—reducing the total number of muscle cells compared with rowing, Nordic track, etc.

Don't forget walking!

Walking can be done all day long. I call walking a "stealth fat-burner" exercise because it is so easy to add hundreds of extra steps a day, especially in small doses. Walking is also an excellent cross training exercise—including treadmill walking. Caution: Don't walk with a long stride.

Cross training for the upper body

Weight training for the bones

While weight work is not a great fat-burning exercise and does not directly benefit running, it can be done on non-running days. You can still do it on running days. Just make sure you wait until after a run. There is a wide range of different ways to build strength. Strength training workouts can be designed to help in strengthening the connections to the spine and other crucial bone support structures. As mentioned previously in this book, weight training for the legs is not recommended.

Older runners need to get advice before beginning weight training

It pays to spend an hour with an experienced strength training expert who can design a program based upon your problems and capabilities. Get advice from an expert before trying any strengthening exercises, including the ones mentioned in this book.

Postural muscle strengthening
—can help to prevent osteoporosis

To reduce the leaning and slumping of the upper body, it helps to build up the muscles that help you stay upright. I do two exercises that have helped me do this quite well. Before doing any exercise, get advice from a physical therapist or knowledgeable strength trainer. Be sure to tell that person about any back or other problems you may have.

The Crunch: Lie on your back, on carpet or any padded surface. Lift your head and upper back slightly off the floor. Go through a narrow range of motion so that you feel your abdominal muscles contracting almost constantly. Start with a few seconds of these, and build up to 30-60 seconds, done 3-5 times a day (one or two days a week).

Arm running: While standing, with hand-held weights (milk jugs, etc), move your arms through a wide range of motion you would use when running—maybe slightly more than usual. Keep the weights close to the body. Start with a few reps and gradually build up to 3-5 sets of 10. Pick a weight that is challenging enough so that you feel exertion at the end of a set of 10. You don't want to struggle during the last few reps.

Ask a strength trainer about exercises that can help you with your needs. Exercises that have helped with spinal connections are the following: shoulder shrug, upright rowing and bench press.

Other exercises that strengthen the upper body...

Swimming:
Although it is not a fat-burner, swimming strengthens the upper body while improving cardiovascular fitness and endurance in those muscles. Swimming can be done on both running days and non-running days.

Push-ups and Pull-ups:
These can build great upper body strength as you innovate to work the upper body muscle groups you want to strengthen.

Don't do these on non-running days!

The following exercises will tire the muscles used for running and keep them from recovering between run days. If you really like to do any of these exercises, you can do them on a short running day after a run. Avoid these completely if you have any pains in the knee or shin.

- Stair machines
- Step aerobics (can cause knee problems)
- Weight training for the leg muscles
- Power walking—especially on a hilly course
- Spinning classes (on a bicycle) in which you stand up on the pedals and push

Cross training can keep you fit, if you must stop running

I know of many runners who have had to take 2 weeks off from running or more, and have not lost noticeable fitness. How? They cross trained. As noted above, the most effective cross training mode for runners is water running.

The key is to do an activity (like water running) that uses the same range of motion used in running. This keeps the neuromuscular system working to capacity.

To maintain conditioning, you must simulate the time and the effort level you would have spent when running. For example, if you were scheduled for a long run that would have taken you 60 minutes, get in the pool and run for 60 minutes. You can take segments of 40-60 seconds in which you reduce your effort (like a walk break), every few minutes, to keep the muscles resilient.

On a speed day, run water segments of about the same length you would have run during those segments on the track or road. Whether going long or fast, try to get up to the same approximate respiration rate that you would have felt when running.

Toys: Heart Rate Monitors and GPS Devices

Heart monitors

Left brain runners who are motivated by technical items and data tracking tell me that they are more motivated when using a heart monitor. Right brain runners who love the intuitive feel of running find that the after-workout number crunching is often too intense, jolting them out of their transcendental state of running. But after talking with hundreds of both types of runners, I realize that there are benefits, especially for "type A" runners and those who are doing speed training.

Heart-rate trainers must determine their max heart rate. It's best to be tested under the supervision of experts. Don't use the tables or formulas. Work off your tested max heart rate (See the section on this issue, below). As you age, the max heart rate will drop. Individuals vary greatly in the amount of the decrease.

Once you determine your maximum heart rate, a good heart monitor can help you manage effort level. This will give you more control over the amount of time you're spending in each level of exertion. This will allow you to reduce overwork and recovery time. As they push into the exertion zone needed on a hard workout, left brain runners will gain a reasonably accurate reading on how much effort to spend or how much they need to back off to avoid a long recovery.

Many "type A" runners have to be told to back off before they injure themselves. I've heard from countless numbers of these runners who feel that the monitors pay for themselves by telling them exactly how slow to run on easy days and how long to rest between speed repetitions during workouts. Right brain runners admit that they enjoy getting verification on the intuitive evaluation of effort levels. The bottom line is that monitors can tell you whether you're going slowly enough to recover, how long to rest during a speed session and what your "red zone" is during a hard speed workout.

All devices have their "technical difficulties." Heart monitors can be influenced by local electronic transmissions and mechanical issues. Cell phone towers and even garage doors can interfere with a monitor on occasion. This is usually an incidental issue. But if you have an abnormal reading—either high or low—it may be due to one of these problems.

Be sure to read the instruction manual thoroughly—particularly concerning how to attach the device to your body for the most accurate reading. If not attached securely you will miss some beats. This means that you are actually working a lot harder than you think you are which can dramatically increase recovery time.

I suggest that you keep monitoring how you feel at each 5% increase toward max heart rate. Over time, you will get better at the intuitive feel, for example, of an 85% effort when you should be at 80%.

Get tested to determine max heart rate

If you are going to use a heart monitor, you should be tested to find your maximum heart rate. Some doctors (especially cardiologists) will do this. Other testing facilities include human performance labs at universities and some health clubs and YMCAs. It is best to have someone supervising the test that is trained in cardiovascular issues. Sometimes the testing facility will misunderstand what you want. Be sure to say that you only need a "max heart rate test"— not a maximum oxygen uptake test. Once you have run for a couple of months with the monitor, you will have a clear idea what your max heart rate is from looking at your heart rate during a series of hard runs. Even on the hard speed workouts, you can usually sense whether you could have worked yourself harder. But until you have more runs that push you to the limits, assume that your current top heart rate is within a beat or two of your current max that has been previously recorded.

Goal: to run faster while keeping the heart rate lower

Use the percentage of max heart rate as your standard
In general, you don't want to get above 90% of max heart rate during workouts. This may happen at the end of a long training program or speed workout, but only for a short period. But your goal is to keep the percentage between 70% and 80% during the first half of the speed workout or longer run, and minimize the upward drift at the end of the workout.

Computing max heart rate percentage
If your max heart rate is 200:
- 90% is 180
- 80% is 160
- 70% is 140
- 65% is 130

On easy days, stay below 65% of max heart rate
When in doubt, run slower. One of the major reasons for fatigue, aches, pains and burnout, is not running slowly enough on the recovery and fun days. This will be noted by a higher than normal heart rate increase at the end of a run. If this happens, slow down and take more walk breaks to keep it below 65%.

Between speed repetitions, let the pulse rate drop below 65% of max before doing another rep
To reduce the "lingering fatigue" that may continue for days after a hard workout, extend the rest interval walk until the heart rate goes down to 65% or lower. At the end of the workout, if the heart rate does not drop below this level for 5 minutes, you should do your warm down and call it a day—*even if you have a few repetitions to go.*

Run smoother on speed repetitions so that your heart rate stays below 80% during speed work
If you really work on running form improvements, you can minimize the heart rate increase by running more efficiently: keeping feet low to the ground, using a light touch, maintaining quick but efficient turnover of the feet. For more info on this, see

the running form chapter in this book, or Galloway's Book on Running 2nd Edition.

Morning pulse

If the chest strap doesn't interfere with your sleep, you can get a very accurate reading on your resting pulse in the morning. This will allow you to monitor over training. Record the low figures each night. Once you establish a baseline, you should take an easy day when the rate rises 5%-9% above this. When it reaches 10% or above, you should take an extra day off. If the heart rate increase is due to an infection, you should not run unless cleared by your doctor.

Use the "two minute rule" for the pace of long runs—not heart rate

Even when running at 65% of max heart rate, many runners will be running a lot faster than they should at the beginning of long runs. Read the guidelines in this book for pacing the long runs, and don't be bashful about running slower.

But at the end of long runs, back off when heart rate exceeds 70% of max

There will be some upward drift of heart rate because of fatigue at the end of long runs. Keep slowing down if this happens, so that you stay around 70% of max HR, or lower—even during the last few miles.

GPS and other distance-pace calculators

There are two types of devices for measuring distance, and both are usually very accurate: GPS and accelerometer technology. While some devices are more accurate than others, most will tell you almost exactly how far you have run. These will allow you to pace your runs from the first tenth of a mile.

Freedom! With these devices, you can run your long runs wherever you wish, instead of having to repeat a loop—just because it is measured. Instead of going to a track to do speed sessions, you can very quickly measure your segments on roads, trails or residential streets. If your goal race is on the track, however, I recommend that at least half of your speed sessions be run on the track. This relates to the principle of training called "specificity."

The GPS devices track your movements by the use of navigational satellites. In general, the more satellites there are, the more accurate the measurement. There are "shadows" where the signals cannot be acquired: buildings, forest or mountains. On trails with lots of small turns, the device may cut the tangents as it accounts for the mileage. These are usually temporary interruptions, but will tend to give a mileage reading that is less than the distance you actually ran.

The accelerometer products require a very easy calibration and have been shown to be very accurate. The "pod" on your shoe is very sensitive to movement and effort, and sends the data to the wrist monitor. I've not heard of any pattern of technical interference with this technology. I've found it best during the calibration to use a variety of paces, taking a walk break or two in order to simulate what you will be doing when you run.

Some devices require batteries; others can be re-charged. Experienced staff members at a technical running store can often advise you on the pros and cons of each product. Sometimes they'll also share the "gossip" on the various brands and models, gained from the feedback they receive from customers.

"Forget about a
personal record when
it's over 60°F"

Dealing with
the Heat

If you slow down a little, on a warm day, you can finish strong, with a higher finish place. That seems obvious, but some runners "lose it" at the beginning of a hot race. The result is a much slower time because of the inevitable slowdown at the end. For every second you run too fast during the first mile of a race on a hot day, you can usually expect to run 2-10 seconds slower at the end.

Heat increases cardiovascular risk. The heart has to work harder even when running slower. Check with your doctor if you have any questions about your risk in this area.

When you exercise strenuously in even moderate heat (above 60°F), you raise core body temperature which triggers a release of blood into the capillaries of your skin to cool you down. This diversion reduces the blood supply available to your exercising muscles, meaning that you will have less blood and less oxygen delivered to the power source that moves you forward. This means there is less blood to move out the waste products from these work sites. The heart is forced to work much harder. As the waste builds up in the muscle, you will slow down.

So the bad news is that in warm weather you are going to feel worse and run slower. The worse news is that working too hard on a hot day could result in a very serious condition called heat disease. Make sure that you read the section on this health problem at the end of this chapter. The good news is that you can adapt to these conditions to some extent, as you learn the best time of the day, clothing and other tricks to keep you cool. Preventive slowdown is best. But it is always better to back off or stop running at the first sign that you may be coming into this condition. The following are proven ways of avoiding heat adversity.

Running the long workouts during summer heat

1. Run before the sun gets above the horizon. Get up early during the warm months and you will avoid most of the extra stress from the radiant effect of the sun. This is particularly a problem in humid areas. Early morning is usually the coolest time of the day. Without having to deal with the sun, most runners can gradually adapt to heat. At the very least, your runs will be more enjoyable than later in the day. Note: Be sure to take care of safety issues.

2. If you must run when the sun is up, pick a shady course. Shade provides a significant relief in areas of low humidity and some relief in humid environments.

3. In areas of low humidity, it's usually cool during the evening and night. In humid environments there may not be much relief. The coolest time of the day when it's humid is just before dawn.

4. Have an indoor facility available. If you use treadmills, you can exercise in air conditioning. If a treadmill bores you, alternate segments of 5-10 minutes—one segment outdoor, and the next indoor.

5. Don't wear a hat! You lose most of your body heat through the top of your head. Covering the head will cause a quicker internal buildup of heat.

6. Wear light clothing, but not cotton. Many of the new, technical fibers (Polypro, Coolmax, DriFit, etc.) will move moisture away from your skin, producing a cooling effect. Cotton soaks up the sweat, making the garment heavier as it sticks to your skin. This means that you won't receive as much of a cooling effect as that provided by the tech products.

7. Pour water over your head. Evaporation not only helps the cooling process—it makes you feel cooler. This psychological boost can make a big difference in motivation, and may help you complete a difficult workout. You can freeze a plastic water bottle overnight and carry it with you on your run.

8. Run the short runs in installments. It is fine, on a hot day when doing a short distance assignment, to put in your 30 minutes by doing 10 in the morning, 10 at noon and 10 at night. The long run, however, should be done at one time. Speed workouts should also be done all at once, but you may take more rest between speed reps, and you may break up the distance when it's hot (running twice as many 800's if you were scheduled for one mile repeats, for example).

9. Take a pool break or a shower chill-down. During a run, it really helps to take a 2-4 minute dip in a pool or a shower. Some runners in hot areas run loops around their neighborhood and let the hose run over the head each lap. The pool is especially helpful in soaking out excess body temperature. I have run in 97 degree temperatures at our Florida running retreat, breaking up a 5 mile run into 3 x 1.7 mile runs. Between each, I take a 2-3 minute "soak break" in the pool and get back out there. It was only at the end of each segment that I got warm again.

10. Sun Screen—a mixed review. Some runners will need to protect themselves. Some products, however, produce a coating on the skin, slowing down the perspiration and producing an increase in body temperature buildup. If you are only in the sun for 30-50 minutes at a time, you may not need to put on sunscreen for cancer protection. Consult with a dermatologist for your specific needs—or find a product that doesn't block the pores.

11. Drink 6-8 oz of a sports drink like Accelerade or water at least every 2 hours, or when thirsty, throughout the day (not when

running) when the weather is hot. Cold water is the best beverage for most during a hot run. Recommended fluid intake is 14-27 oz. an hour during exercise.

12. Look at the clothing thermometer at the end of this section. Wear loose fitting garments that have some texture in the fabric. Texture will limit or prevent the perspiration from causing a clinging effect that limits the coolness of evaporation.

13. When the temperature is above 90°F, you have my permission to re-arrange your running shoes—preferably in an air conditioned environment.

Hot weather slowdown for long runs

As the temperature rises above 55°F (12°C), your body starts to build up heat, but most runners aren't significantly slowed until 60°F (14°C). If you make the adjustments early, you won't have to suffer later and slow down a lot more at that time. The baseline for this table is 60°F or 14°C.

* Adjust pace for heat:
    50-60 year olds: 30 sec per mile slower for every 5 degrees above 60°F (20 sec/km for ea 2°C above 14°C)
    61-70 year olds: 35 sec per mile slower for every 5 degrees above 60°F (25 sec/km for ea 2°C above 14°C)
    71-80 year olds: 45 sec per mile slower for every 5 degrees above 60°F (33 sec/km for ea 2°C above 14°C)
    81-90 year olds: 60 sec per mile slower for every 5 degrees above 60°F (45 sec/km for ea 2°C above 14°C)
    91 +: Limit long runs to no more than 10-12 miles (15-20K) and follow formula for 80-90 year olds.

Heat disease alert!

While it is unlikely that you will push yourself into heat disease, the longer you are exercising in hot (and/or humid) conditions, the more you increase the likelihood of this dangerous medical situation. That's why I recommend breaking up your exercise into short segments when you run outdoors in the heat. Be sensitive to your reactions to the heat and those of the runners around you. When experiencing one of the symptoms, it is normally not a major problem unless there is significant distress. But when several are experienced, take action because heat disease can lead to death. It's always better to be conservative by stopping the workout and cooling off.

Note: Those who have cardiovascular disease or a family history of it, or have significant risk factors should avoid hot weather running completely.

Symptoms:

- Intense heat build-up in the head
- General overheating of the body
- Significant headache
- Significant nausea
- General confusion and loss of concentration
- Loss of muscle control
- Excessive sweating and then cessation of sweating
- Clammy skin
- Excessively rapid breathing
- Muscle cramps
- Feeling faint
- Unusual heart beat or rhythm

Heat disease risk factors:

- Viral or bacterial infection
- Taking medication—especially cold medicines, diuretics, medicines for diarrhea, antihistamines, atropine, scopolamine, tranquilizers and even cholesterol and blood pressure medications. Check with your doctor on medication issues— especially when running in hot weather.
- Dehydration (especially due to alcohol)
- Severe sunburn
- Overweight
- Lack of heat training

- Exercising more than one is used to
- Occurrence of heat disease in the past
- Two or more nights of extreme sleep deprivation
- Certain medical conditions including high cholesterol, high blood pressure, extreme stress, asthma, Diabetes, epilepsy, cardiovascular disease, smoking and a general lack of fitness.
- Drug use, including alcohol, over-the-counter medications, prescription drugs, etc., (consult with your doctor about using drugs when you are exercising hard in hot weather).

Take action! Call 911

Use your best judgement, but in most cases anyone who exhibits two or more of the symptoms should get into a cool environment and get medical attention immediately. An extremely effective cool-off method is to soak towels, sheets or clothing in cool or cold water and wrap them around the individual. If ice is available, sprinkle some ice over the wet cloth.

Heat adaptation workout

If you regularly force yourself to deal with body heat buildup, you will adapt somewhat to the stress. While you'll never feel comfortable, you can complete warm weather runs with strength, be more competitive (if you wish) in races and recover faster when you maintain your heat adaptations. As with all training components, it is important to do this regularly. You should be sweating to some extent at the end of the workout, although the amount and the duration of perspiration is an individual issue. If the heat is particularly oppressive, cut back the amount. Don't let yourself get into the beginning stages of heat disease. Get a doctor's clearance before doing this. Those who have cardiovascular risk factors should not do this workout.

Important note: Read the section on heat disease and stop this workout if you sense that you are even beginning to become nauseous, lose concentration or mental awareness of your condition, etc.

The workout:
- Do this workout on a short running day once a week.
- Do the run-walk ratio that you usually use, going at a very easy pace.
- Warm up with a 5 min walk and take a 5 min walk warm down.
- Temperature should be between 75°F and 85°F (22-27°C) for best results.
- Stop at the first sign of nausea or significant heat stress or other symptoms of heat disease.
- When below 70°F (19°C), you can put on additional layers of clothing to simulate a higher temperature.
- First session: run-walk for only 3-4 minutes in the heat.
- Each successive session: add 2-3 minutes.
- Build up to a maximum of 25 minutes—but don't push into heat disease.
- Regularity is important to maintain adaptations. Do this once every week.
- If you miss a week or more, reduce the amount significantly and rebuild.

Tip: Maintaining heat tolerance during the winter

By adding more layers of clothing than you need, you can maintain much of your summer heat conditioning that took so much work to produce. The layers should cause you to sweat within the first 4-6 minutes of your run-walk. Continue to run for a total of 12 minutes or more as you build according to the sidebar above.

Troubleshooting
Performance

Times are slowing down at the end
- Your long runs aren't long enough or slow enough.
- You are running too fast at the beginning of the race (older runners often have dramatic negative splits).
- Walk breaks need to be taken more frequently.
- You may be over trained; back off the speed sessions for a week or two—run every other day.
- In speed workouts, run slower in the beginning and run hardest at the end of the workout.
- Cut the distance of the speed rep in half, and run twice as many reps.
- Temperature and/or humidity may be to blame. Try slowing down at the beginning.

Slowing down in the middle of the race
- You may be running too hard at the beginning. Slow down during the first third of your race by a few seconds each mile.
- Take more frequent walk breaks.
- In speed workouts, run slower in the beginning and work the harder in the middle of the workout.

Nauseous at the end
- You ran too fast at the beginning.
- Temperature is above 65°F/17°C.
- You ate too much (or drank too much) before the race or workout.
- You ate the wrong foods—most commonly, fat, fried foods, milk products and fibrous foods.
- You ate or drank too much during the run.
- Since sports drinks cause nausea during runs, use water for your fluid replacement.

Tired during workouts
- Low in B vitamins
- Low in iron—have a serum ferritin test
- Not eating enough protein

- Blood sugar is low before exercise—eat more often during the day, and have a snack 30-60 min before
- Not eating within 30 min of the finish of a previous run (to restock muscle glycogen)
- Eating too much fat—especially before or right after a run
- Running too many days per week
- Running too hard on long runs
- Running too hard on all running days
- Not taking enough walk breaks from the beginning of your runs

Reasons why you may not be improving:

1. You're over-trained, and tired—if so, reduce your training, and/or take an extra rest day.
2. You may have chosen a goal that is too ambitious for your current ability
3. You may have missed some of your workouts or not been as regular with your training.
4. The temperature may have been above 60°F (14°C). Above this, you will slow down (the longer the race, the greater the effect of increased heat).
5. When using different test courses, one of them may not have been accurately measured.
6. You ran the first third of the workout or the race too fast.

Problems and Solutions

Side pain

This is very common, and usually has a simple fix. Normally it is nothing to worry about...it just hurts. This condition is due to two things: the lack of deep breathing, and going a little too fast from the beginning of the run. You can correct #2 easily by walking more at the beginning, and/or slowing down your running pace during the first few minutes of running.

Deep breathing from the beginning of a run can prevent side pain. This way of inhaling air is performed by diverting the air you breathe into your lower lungs. Also called "belly breathing," this is how we breathe when asleep, and it provides maximum opportunity for oxygen absorption. If you don't deep breathe when you run, and you are not getting the oxygen you need it, the side pain will tell you. By slowing down, walking, and breathing deeply for a while, the pain may go away. But sometimes it does not. Most runners just continue to run and walk with the side pain. In 50 years of running and helping others run, I've not seen any lasting negative effect due to running with a side pain—it just hurts.

*Tip: **Some runners have found that side pain goes away if they tightly grasp a rock in the hand that is on the side of the pain. Squeeze it for 15 seconds or so. Keep squeezing 3-5 times as you breathe deeply.***

You don't have to take a maximum breath to perform this technique. Simply breathe a normal breath but send it to the lower lungs. You know that you have done this if your stomach goes up and down as you inhale and exhale. If your chest goes up and down, you are breathing shallowly.

Note: never breathe in and out rapidly. This can lead to hyperventilation, dizziness and fainting.

I feel great one day...and not the next

If you can solve this problem, you could become a very wealthy person. There are a few common reasons for this, but there will always be "those days" when the body doesn't seem to work right or the gravity seems heavier than normal—and you cannot find a reason. You should keep looking for the causes of your letdowns in your journal. If you feel this way several times a week, for two or more weeks in a row, you may need more rest in your program or possibly a medical checkup.

1. Just do it. In most cases, this is a one-day occurrence. Most runners just put more walking into the mix, slow down and get through it. Before doing a speed workout, however, make sure that there's not a medical reason for the "bad" feeling. I've had some of my best workouts after feeling very bad during the first few miles—or the first few speed repetitions.

2. Heat and/or humidity will make you feel worse. You will often feel better when the temperature is below 60°F (14°C) and miserable when 75°F (21.5°C) or above—and/or the humidity is high.

3. Low blood sugar can make any run a bad run. You may feel good at the start and suddenly feel like you have no energy. Every step seems to take a major effort. Read the section in this book on blood sugar.

4. Low motivation. Use the rehearsal techniques in the "mental toughness" chapter to get you out the door on a bad day—or to help you continue running on a tough day. These have helped numerous runners turn their minds around, even in the middle of a run.

5. Infection can leave you feeling lethargic, achy and unable to run at the same pace that was easy a few days earlier. Check the normal signs (fever, chills, swollen lymph glands, higher morning pulse rate, etc.) and at least call your doctor if you suspect something.

6. Medication and alcohol, even when taken the day before, can leave a hangover that may not affect any area of your life except for your running. Your doctor or pharmacist should be able to tell you about the effect of medication on strenuous exercise.

7. A slower start can make the difference between a good day and a bad day. When your body is on the edge of fatigue or other stress, just 5-10 seconds too fast per mile, walking and/or running, can push into discomfort or worse. A quick adjustment to a slightly slower pace before you get too tired can turn this around.

8. Caffeine can help because it gets the central nervous system working to top capacity. I feel better and my legs work much better when I have had a cup of coffee an hour before the start of a run. Of course, those who have any problems with caffeine should avoid it or consult a doctor.

9. Take an extra day off each week, especially if you're running 4 or more days per week.

Cramps in the muscles

At some point, most people who run will experience an isolated cramp. These muscle contractions usually occur in the feet or the calf muscles and may come during a run or walk. They could also hit afterward at random. Most commonly, they will occur at night or when you are sitting at your desk or watching TV in the afternoon or evening. When severe cramps occur during a run, you will have to stop or significantly slow down.

Cramps vary in severity. Most are mild but some can grab so hard that they shut down the muscles and hurt when they seize up. Relax the muscle. Try to lightly massage the cramp. This can help to bring most of the cramps around. Odds are that stretching will make the cramp worse or tear the muscle fibers.

Most cramps are due to overuse—doing more than in the recent past, or continuing to put yourself at your limit, especially in warm weather. Look at the pace and distance of your runs and workouts in your training journal to see if you have been running too far, or too fast, or both. Remember to adjust pace for heat: 30 sec/mile slower for each 5 degrees (F) of temperature increase above 60°F— or 20 sec/kilometer for every 2 degrees C of temperature increase above 14°F.

- Continuous running increases cramping. Taking walk breaks more often can reduce or eliminate them. Several runners who used to cramp when they ran continuously stopped cramping with a 1 minute walk break after 1-3 minutes of running during a long or fast run.

- During hot weather, a good electrolyte beverage (consumed during the day, throughout the day) can help to replace the salts that your body loses in sweating. A drink like Accelerade, for example, can help to replace these minerals when you drink 6-8 oz every 1-2 hours, throughout the day.

- On very long hikes, walks or runs, however, the continuous sweating, especially when drinking a lot of fluid, can push your sodium levels too low and produce muscle cramping. If this happens regularly, a buffered salt tablet, such as Succeed, can help. If you have any blood pressure or other sodium issues, check with your doctor first.

- Many medications, especially those designed to lower cholesterol, have muscle cramps as one of their known side effects. Runners who use medications and suffer from cramps should ask their doctor about this issue and investigate alternatives.

Here are several ways of dealing with cramps:

1. Take a longer and gentler warm-up.
2. Shorten your run segment, increase the walk segment or take walk breaks more often.
3. Slow down your walk.
4. Shorten your distance on a hot/humid day.
5. Break your run up into two segments (but not long runs or speed workouts).
6. Look at any other exercise that could be causing the cramps.
7. Take a buffered salt tablet at the beginning of your exercise.
8. Don't push off as hard or bounce as high off the ground.
9. During speed workouts on hot days, walk more during the rest interval.

Note: if you have high blood pressure or similar problem, ask your doctor before taking any salt product.

Upset stomach or diarrhea

Sooner or later, virtually every runner has at least one episode of nausea or diarrhea. It comes from the buildup of total stress that you accumulate in your life—and specifically the stress of the workout. But stress is the result of many unique conditions within the individual. Your body produces the nausea/diarrhea to get you to reduce the exercise, which will reduce the stress. Here are the common causes:

1. **Running too fast or too far is the most common cause.** Runners are confused about this because the pace doesn't feel too fast in the beginning. Each person has a level of fatigue that triggers these conditions. Slowing down and taking more walk breaks will help you manage the problem. Speed training and racing will increase stress quickly.

2. **Eating too much or too soon before the run.** Your system has to work hard when running, and it is also hard work to digest food. Doing both at the same time raises stress and results in nausea,

etc. Having partially-digested food in your stomach is an extra stress and a likely target for elimination.

3. **Eating a high fat or high protein diet.** Even one meal that has over 50% of the calories in fat or protein can lead to nausea/diarrhea (N/D) hours later when you run.

4. **Eating too much the afternoon or evening, the day before.** A big evening meal will still be in the gut the next morning. When you bounce up and down during a run, which you will, you add stress to the system, sometimes resulting in N/D.

5. **Heat and humidity are a major cause of these problems.** Some people don't adapt well to even modest heat increases and experience N/D when racing (or during speed sessions) at the same pace that did not produce the problem in cool weather. In hot conditions, everyone has a core body temperature increase that will result in significant stress to the system—often causing nausea, and sometimes diarrhea. You can manage this better by slowing down, taking more walk breaks and pouring water over your head.

6. Drinking too much water before a run. If you have too much water in your stomach, you put stress on the digestive system. Reduce your intake to the bare minimum. Most runners don't need to drink any fluid before a run that is 60 minutes or less.

7. Drinking too much of a sugar/electrolyte drink. Water is the easiest substance for the body to process. The addition of sugar and/or electrolyte minerals, as in a sports drink, makes the substance harder to digest. During a run (especially on a hot day), it is best to drink only water if you have had N/D or other problems. Cold water is best. But even too much water can upset the system.

8. Drinking too much fluid (especially a sugar drink) too soon after a run. Even if you are very thirsty, don't gulp down large quantities of any fluid during a short period of time after a run. Try to drink no more than 6-8 oz, every 20 minutes. If you are particularly prone to N/D, just take 2-4 sips, every 5 minutes. When the body is stressed and tired, it's not a good idea to consume a sugar drink (sports drink, etc). The extra stress of digesting the sugar can lead to problems.

9. Don't let running be stressful to you. Some runners get too obsessed about getting their run in or running at a specific pace. This adds stress to your life. Relax and let your run diffuse some of the other tensions in your life. When you are under a lot of "life stress" it's OK to delay a speed workout when the thought of fast running seems to increase your stress level. Take an easy jog! You should be in charge—not some training schedule.

Note: if you are experiencing frequent N/D without cause, see your physician.

Headache

There are several reasons why runners get headaches on runs. While uncommon, they happen to the average runner about 1-5 times a year. The extra stress that running puts on the body can trigger a headache on a tough day. This happens even though you are relaxing during the run. Many runners find that one dose of an over-the-counter headache medication takes care of the problem. As always, consult with your doctor about use of medication. Here are some of the causes/solutions:

Dehydration—if you run in the morning, make sure that you hydrate well the day before. Avoid alcohol if you run in the mornings and have headaches. Also watch the salt in your dinner meal the night before (or too much salt all day long) if you are experiencing headaches. A good sports drink like Accelerade, taken throughout the previous day, will help to keep your fluid levels and your electrolytes "topped off." If you run in the afternoon, follow the same advice leading up to your run, on the day of the run. If you are dehydrated an hour before a run, it doesn't help to drink a huge amount of water at that time—6-8 oz is fine.

Medications can often produce dehydration. There are some medications that make runners more prone to headaches. Check with your doctor.

It's too hot for you: Run at a cooler time of the day (usually in the morning before the sun gets above the horizon). When on a hot run, pour water over your head.

Being in the sun: Try to stay in the shade as much as possible. Wear a visor not a hat, making sure the band is not too tight. When the temperature rises above 60°F, don't cover the top of your head.

Running a little too fast: Start all runs more slowly and walk more during the first half of the run.

Running farther than you have run in the recent past: Monitor your mileage and don't increase more than about 15% farther than you have run on any single run in the recent past. When increasing (or when running any long run), be sure to run at least 2 min/mi slower than you could legitimately run for a marathon (see the "magic mile" segment in this book).

Low blood sugar level: be sure that you boost your BLS with a snack about 30-60 min before you run. If you are used to having it, caffeine in a beverage can sometimes help this situation also—but caffeine causes headaches for a small percentage of runners.

If prone to migraines: Generally avoid caffeine, and try your best to avoid dehydration. Talk to your doctor about other possibilities.

Watch your neck and lower back: If you have a slight forward lean as you run, you can put pressure on the spine, particularly in the neck and lower back. Read the form chapter in this book and run upright.

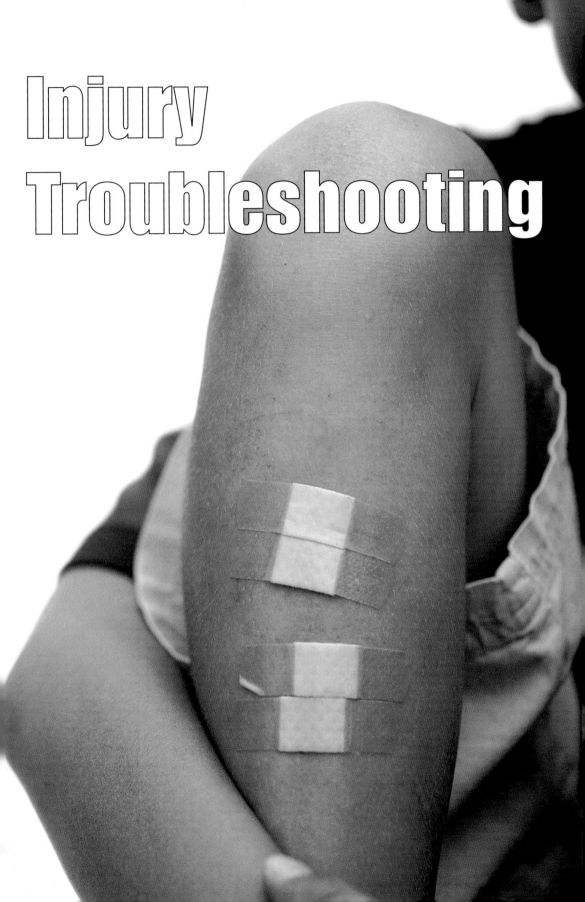

Injury
Troubleshooting

Quick treatment tips

For all injuries:

1. Take 3 days off from running or any activity that could aggravate the area.
2. Avoid any activity that could aggravate the injury site.
3. As you return to running, stay below the threshold of further irritation with much more liberal walking.
4. Don't stretch unless you have Ilio-Tibial band injury. Stretching interferes with the healing of most injuries and often increases the healing time.

Muscle injuries:

1. Call your doctor's office and see if you can take prescription-strength anti-inflammatory medication. Always follow your doctor's advice about medication.
2. See a sports massage therapist who has worked successfully on many runners. Deep tissue massage can speed up muscle recovery.
3. If you experience no improvement after 4 days of not running, call an orthopedist and set up an appointment.

Tendon and foot injuries

1. Rub a chunk of ice directly on the area for 15 minutes every night (keep rubbing until the area gets numb—about 15 minutes).

   Note: ice bags and gel ice don't seem to do any good.

2. Foot injuries sometimes are helped by an air cast at first. This can stabilize the foot or leg so that the healing can begin.

Knee injuries

1. Call your doctor's office to see if you can take prescription-strength anti-inflammatory medication.
2. Try gentle walking, on your running days, for a week or two. Sometimes this will allow the knee to heal while walking maintains a lot of the conditioning.

3. Sometimes knee straps (available at many running stores) can relieve pain. Ask your doctor. In most cases, you must try these to see if they help.
4. Get a shoe check to see if you are wearing the right pair (if you over-pronate, a motion-control shoe may help).
5. If you over pronate, an orthotic may help.
6. If you have internal knee pain, a glucosamine supplement may help (usually takes 6-8 weeks to take effect).

Shin injuries

1. Rule out a stress fracture. In this case, the pain usually gets worse as you run, but check with your doctor. You should not run if you have any type of fracture.
2. If the pain gradually goes away as you run, there is less worry of a stress fracture. This is probably a shin splint. If you stay below the threshold of activity that irritates the shin muscle, you can run with shin splints as they gradually go away (check with doctor to be sure).
3. Take more walk breaks, run more slowly, etc.

Running while healing

With most running injuries, you can continue to run while the injury is healing. But first, you must take some time away from running to get the healing started. If you do this at the beginning of an injury, you only need 2-5 days off. The longer you try to push through the problem, the more damage is caused and the longer it will take to heal. Stay in touch with the doctor at any stage of this healing/running process, follow his/her advice and use your best judgement.

To allow for healing—once you have returned to running—stay below the threshold of further irritation. In other words, if the injury feels slightly irritated after running 2.5 miles, and starts hurting more after 3 miles, you should run no more than 2 miles. And if your "healthy" run-walk ratio is 3 min run/1 min walk, you should drop back to 1/1 or 30 seconds/30 seconds, or 30 seconds run/60 seconds walk.

Always allow a day of rest between running days. With most injuries you can cross train to maintain conditioning, but make sure that your injury will allow this. Again, your doctor can advise.

Best cross training modes to maintain your running conditioning

Before doing any of these ask your doctor. Most are fine for most injuries. But some carry the risk of irritating the injured area and delaying the healing process. For more information on this, see the chapter on cross training in my Galloway's Book on Running, 2nd Edition. Gradually build up the cross training because you have to also gradually condition those muscles. Even walking is a great way to maintain conditioning if the injury and the doctor will allow it.

1. Running in the water (can improve your running form)
2. Nordic track machines
3. Walking
4. Rowing machines
5. Elliptical machines

There is much more information on specific injuries in my *Galloway's Book on Running*, 2nd Edition. But here are my suggestions:

Treatment suggestions —from one runner to another

Knee pain

Most knee problems will go away if you stop running immediately (don't run the last mile) and take 5 days off. Ask your doctor if you can use anti-inflammatory medication. Try to figure out what caused the knee problem. Make sure that your running courses don't have a slant or canter. Look at the most worn pair of shoes you have, even walking shoes. If there is wear on the inside of the forefoot, you probably over pronate. If you have repeat issues with knee pain, you may need a foot support or orthotics. If there is pain under the kneecap, or arthritis, the glucosamine/chondroitin products have helped. The best I've found in this category is Joint Maintenance Product by Cooper Complete.

Outside of the knee pain—ilio-tibial band syndrome

This band of fascia acts as a tendon on the outside of the leg from the hip to just below the knee. The pain is most commonly noticed on the outside of the knee, but can occur anywhere along the band. I believe this to be a "wobble injury." When the running muscles

get tired, they don't keep you on a straight running track. The I-T band tries to restrain the wobbling motion, but it cannot. By continuing to run, your wobbling motion will overuse the band. Most of the feedback I receive from runners and doctors is that once the healing has started (usually a few days off from running), most runners will heal just as fast when continuing to run or completely laying off. In this case, however, it is crucial to get your doctor's OK to run, and then, to stay below the threshold of further irritation.

Treatment for ilio-tibial band:

1. Stretching: Stretching the I-T band releases the tightness that produces the pain. With this injury, you can stretch before, after and even during a run. The primary role for stretching is to allow you to run when the band tightens.

2. Self-massage using a foam roller. This device has helped thousands of runners get over I-T band problems. On my website, www.RunInjury Free.com, there is a picture of someone using a foam roller. Put the roller on the floor and lie on it using body weight to press and roll the area that is sore. Rolling before a run will help it warm up, and rolling afterward often helps the injury recover faster.

3. Massage Therapy: A good massage therapist can tell whether massage will help and where to massage. The two areas for possible attention are the connecting points of the connective tissue that is tight, and the fascia band itself, in several places. "The stick" is a self massage roller device that has also helped many runners recover from I-T band problems as they run. As with the foam roller, it helps to warm up the area before a run, and to roll it out afterward.

4. Walking: Maintain a short stride.

5. Direct ice massage on the area of pain: 15 minutes of continuous rubbing every night.

Shin pain—"Shin splints" or stress fracture

Almost always, pain in this area indicates a minor irritation called "shin splints" that allows running and walking as you heal. The greatest pain or irritation during injury is during the start of a run or walk, which gradually lessens or goes away as you run and walk. It takes several weeks (minimum) to fully heal, so you must have patience.

Inside pain: posterior shin splints. Irritation of the inside of the leg coming up from the ankle is called "posterior tibia shin splints" and is often due to over pronation of the foot (foot rolls in at push off).

Front of shin: anterior shin splints. When the pain is in the muscle on the front of the lower leg it is "anterior tibia shin splints." This is very often due to having too long a stride when running and especially when walking. Downhill terrain should be avoided as much as possible during the healing process.

Stress Fracture: If the pain is in a very specific place, and increases as you run, you could have a more serious problem: a stress fracture. This is becoming increasingly more common in mature athletes who do speed training and who run more than 3 days a week. It also happens to those who do too much, too soon. Stress fractures can indicate low bone density and calcium deficiency. If you even suspect a stress fracture, do not run or do anything stressful on the leg and see a doctor. Stress fractures take weeks of no running and usually require wearing a cast for the first few weeks.

Heel pain—plantar fascia

"The most effective treatment is putting your foot in a supportive shoe before your 1st step in the morning."

This very common injury (pain on the inside or center of the heel) is felt when you first walk on the foot in the morning. As you get warmed up, it gradually goes away, only to return the next morning. The most important treatment is to put your foot in a supportive shoe before you step out of bed. Be sure to get a "shoe check" at a technical running store to make sure that you have the right shoe for your foot. If the pain is felt during the day, and is painful, you should consult with a podiatrist. Usually the doctor will construct a foot support that will surround your arch and heel. This does not always need to be a hard orthotic. Usually a softer one, designed for your foot, works quite well.

The "toe squincher" exercise can help develop foot strength that will also support the foot. This is simply done by pointing your toes and contracting your foot for several seconds until it almost cramps. It takes several weeks for this to take effect. This is another injury that allows for running as you heal, but stay in touch with your doctor.

Gout—toe joint pain (ankle, foot tenderness) with swelling

The swelling of the big toe joint, with pain, is the result of an accumulation of uric acid in your foot. The pain may also be felt in the ankle, with significant and often debilitating tenderness on the bottom of the forefoot. Major causes are alcohol consumption, too much protein (particularly red meat), and being dehydrated. There are some effective drugs that can manage this problem.

Back of the foot—achilles tendon

The achilles tendon is the narrow band of tendon rising up from the heel and connecting to the calf muscle. It is part of a very efficient mechanical system, which performs like a strong rubber band. The resulting action will leverage a lot of spring out of the foot, with little effort from the calf muscle. It is usually injured because of excessive stretching, either through running or by stretching exercises. First, avoid any activity that stretches the tendon in any way. It helps to add a small heel lift to all shoes, which reduces the range of motion. Every night, rub a chunk of ice directly on the tendon. Keep rubbing for about 15 minutes, until the tendon gets numb. Bags of ice or frozen gels don't do any good in my opinion. Usually after 3-5 days off from running, the icing takes hold and the achilles feels stronger each day. It has been my experience that anti-inflammatory medication very rarely helps with the achilles tendon.

Hip and groin pain

There are a variety of elements that could be aggravated in the hip area. Since the hips are not prime movers in running, they are usually abused when you continue to push on when leg muscles are very tired. The hips may be forced to do more work and must take on more extraneous motion for which they are not designed. Ask your doctor about prescription-strength anti-inflammatory medication, as this can often speed up recovery. Avoid stretching and any activity that aggravates the area.

Calf muscle

The calf is the most important muscle for running. It is often irritated by speed work, and can be pushed into injury by stretching, running too fast when tired, too many speed sessions without adequate rest in between and sprinting at the end of races or workouts.

Deep tissue massage has been the best treatment for most calf muscle problems experienced by my athletes and myself. Try to find an experienced massage therapist who has helped lots of runners with calf problems. This can be painful but is sometimes the only way to remove some bio-damage in the muscle. The "stick" can be very beneficial for working damage out of the calf muscle on a daily basis (see our website for more information on this product).

Don't stretch! Stretching will tear the muscle fibers that are trying to heal. Avoid running hills, and take very frequent walk breaks as you return to running.

Choosing the Best Shoe for You

The best advice I can give you is to get the best advice. If you have a good technical running store in your area, go there. The advice from experienced shoe fitters will be priceless, especially if you have some individual foot issues, as do most runners over 49 years old. Here are some other helpful tips:

First, look at the wear pattern on your most worn pair of walking or running shoes. Use the guide below to help you choose among 3-4 pairs of shoes:

Floppy feet

Floppy feet produce spots of wear. Be particularly aware of wear on the inside of the forefoot. If you have spots of wear, and have some foot or knee pain, try some of the shoes that have minimal cushion, or are designed for motion control.

Overpronated foot

This wear pattern shows significant wear on the inside of the forefoot. If you have knee or hip pain, look for a shoe that has "structure" or motion-control capabilities. If you don't have pain, look at a neutral shoe that does not have a lot of cushion in the forefoot.

Rigid

If you have a wear pattern on the outside of the forefoot of the shoe, and no wear on the inside, you probably have a rigid foot and can choose a neutral shoe that has adequate cushion and flexibility for you, as you run and walk in them.

If you can't tell...

Choose shoes that are neutral or that have a mid range of cushion and support.

Shoe selection tips

1. Set aside at least 30 minutes to choose your next shoe, as you compare the 3 candidates you have chosen.
2. Bring with you your most worn pair of shoes, foot supports, socks used, and a pair of shoes that work well for you.
3. Run and walk on a pavement surface and notice the difference in various shoes. If you have a floppy foot, make sure that you get the support you need.
4. You want a shoe that feels natural on your foot—no pressure or aggravation—while allowing the foot to go through the range of motion needed for running. Runners that need motion control should feel more firm support from the shoe.
5. Again, take as much time as you need before deciding.
6. If the store doesn't let you run in the shoe, go to another store.

Go by how they fit and not the size noted on the box of the shoe. Most runners wear a running shoe that is about 2 sizes larger than their street shoes. For example, I wear a size 10 street shoe but run in a size 12 running model. Be open to getting the best fit, regardless of what size is printed on the box.

Extra room for your toes

Your foot tends to swell during the day, so it's best to fit shoes after noon. Be sure to stand up in the shoe during the fitting process and measure how much extra room you have in the toe region. Go with the size that feels comfortable on the largest of your feet.

Width issues

- Running shoes tend to be a bit wider than street shoes.
- Usually, by tightening the laces you can "snug up" the difference, if your foot is a bit narrower.
- The shoe shouldn't be laced too tight around your foot because the foot swells during running and walking. On hot days, the average runner will move up one-half shoe size. Again, leave extra room at the end of each shoe.
- In general, running shoes are designed to handle a certain amount of "looseness." But if you are getting blisters when wearing a loose shoe, tighten the laces.

- Some shoe companies have selected shoes in widths.
- The shoe is too narrow if you are rolling off the edge of the shoe as you push off on either side.

Shoes for women

Women's shoes tend to be slightly narrower than those for men, and the heel is usually a bit smaller. The quality of the major running shoe brands is the same in men's and women's models. About 25% of women runners have feet that can fit better into men's shoes. Usually the confusion comes when women wear large sizes. The better running stores can help you deal with the issues in this area.

Breaking in a new shoe

- Wear the new shoe around the house for an hour or more each day for a week. If you stay on carpet, and the shoe doesn't fit correctly, you can exchange it at the store. But if you have put some wear on the shoe, dirt, etc., few stores will take it back.
- In most cases you will find that the shoe feels comfortable enough to run immediately. It is best to continue walking in the shoe, gradually allowing the foot to adjust to the heel, the ankle pads, and to make other adjustments. If you run in the shoe too soon, blisters are often the result.
- If there are no rubbing issues on the foot when walking, you could walk in the new shoe for a gradually increasing amount, for 2-4 days.
- On the first run, just run about half a mile in the shoe. Put on your old shoes and continue the run.
- On each successive run, increase the distance run in the new shoe for 3-4 runs. At this point, you will usually have the new shoe broken in.

How do you know when it's time to get a new shoe?

1. When you have been using a shoe for 3-4 weeks successfully, buy another pair of exactly the same model, make, size, etc. The reason for this: The shoe companies often make significant changes or discontinue shoe models (even successful ones) about every 6-8 months.

2. Walk around the house in the new shoe for a few days.
3. After the shoe feels broken in, run the first half mile of one of your weekly runs (shoe break-in day) in the new shoe, then put on the shoe that is already broken in.
4. On this weekly shoe comparison, gradually run a little more in the new shoe.
5. Several weeks later you will notice that the new shoe offers more bounce than the old one.
6. Shift to the new pair before the original one is worn out. When you're not getting good support from the original shoe, you can increase the chance of injury.
7. Start breaking in a third pair.

The Clothing Thermometer

After years of coaching runners in various climates, here are my recommendations for the appropriate clothing based upon the temperature. The first layer, since it will be next to your skin, should feel comfortable, and should be designed to move the moisture away from your skin. You may have to resist the temptation to buy a fashion color—function is most important. As you try on the clothing in the store, watch for seams and extra material in areas where you will have body parts rubbing together (armpit, between legs).

Cotton is usually not a good fabric for those who perspire a great deal. This fabric absorbs the sweat, holding it next to your skin, and increases the weight you must carry during the run. Garments made out of fabric labeled Polypro, Coolmax, Drifit, etc., can retain enough body heat to keep you warm in winter, while releasing the extra amount. By moving moisture to the outside of the garment, these technical fabrics help you stay cooler in summer, while avoiding the winter chill.

Temperature	What to wear
14°C or 60°F and above	Tank top, or singlet, and shorts
9 to13°C or 50 to 59°F	T-shirt and shorts
5 to 8°C or 40 to 49°F	Long sleeve light-weight shirt, shorts or tights (or nylon long pants), Mittens and gloves
0 to 4°C or 30 to 39°F	Long sleeve medium weight shirt, and another T-shirt, tights and shorts, socks, mittens or gloves, and a hat over the ears
-4 to –1°C or 20-29°F	Medium-weight long sleeve shirt, another T shirt, tights and shorts, socks, mittens or gloves, and a hat over the ears
-8 to –3°C or 10-19°F	Medium-weight long sleeve shirt, and medium/heavy weight shirt, tights and shorts, nylon wind suit, top and pants, socks, thick mittens, and a hat over the ears

-12 to –7°C or 0-9°F	Two medium- to heavy-weight long sleeve tops, thick tights, thick underwear (especially for men), medium to heavy warm up, gloves and thick mittens, ski mask, a hat over the ears, and Vaseline covering any exposed skin
-18 to –11°C or –15°F	Two heavy-weight long sleeve tops, tights and thick tights, thick underwear (and supporter for men), thick warm up (top and pants), mittens over gloves, thick ski mask and a hat over ears, Vasoline covering any exposed skin, thicker socks on your feet and other foot protection, as needed.
-20 both °C & °F	Add layers as needed

What not to wear

1. A heavy coat in winter. If the layer is too thick, you'll heat up, sweat excessively and cool too much when you take it off.
2. No shirt for men in summer. Fabric that holds some of the moisture will give you more of a cooling effect as you run and walk.
3. Too much sun screen. It can interfere with sweating
4. Socks that are too thick in summer. Your feet swell and the pressure from the socks can increase the chance of a black toenail and blisters.
5. Lime green shirt with bright pink polka dots (unless you have a lot of confidence and/or can run fast).

Special cases:

Chaffing can be reduced by lycra and other fabric. Many runners have eliminated chaffing between the legs by using a lycra (bike tight) as an undergarment. These are also called "lycra shorts." There are also several skin lubricants on the market, including Glide.

Some men suffer from irritation of their nipples. Having a slick and smooth fabric across the chest will reduce this. There is now a product called Nip-Guard that has virtually eliminated this problem.

Products that Enhance Running

The following products will help all runners. Because recovery continues to slow down with each passing year, older runners will benefit even more from use of the following. For more information on these, visit ***www.JeffGalloway.com***.

Other Galloway books, training schedules, and gifts that keep on giving—even to yourself

(Order them, autographed, from www.JeffGalloway.com)

Walking: Walkers now have a book that explains the many benefits, how to maximize them with training programs for 5K, 10K, half and full marathons. There is resource information on fat-burning, nutrition, motivation and much more.

Getting Started: This is more than a state-of-the-art book for beginners. It gently takes walkers into running, with a 6 month schedule that has been very successful. Also included is information on fat-burning, nutrition, motivation, and body management. This is a great gift for your friends or relatives who can be "infected" positively by running.

A Year-Round Plan: You'll find daily workouts for 52 weeks and three levels of runners: to finish, to maximize potential, and time improvement. It has the long runs, speed sessions and drills, hill sessions all listed in the order needed to do a 5K, 10K, half and full marathon during one year. Resource material is included to help with many running issues.

Galloway's Book on Running, 2nd Edition: This is the best-seller among running books since 1984. Thoroughly revised and expanded in 2001, you'll find training programs for 5K, 10K, and half marathons with nutrition, fat-burning, walk breaks, motivation, injuries, shoes and much more. This is a total resource book.

Marathon: This has the information you need to train for the classic event. There are training programs with details on walk breaks, long runs, marathon nutrition, mental marathon toughness and much more.

Half Marathon: This new book provides highly successful and detailed training schedules for various time goals. Information is provided on nutrition, mental preparation, fluids, race day logistics and check lists and much more.

Testing Yourself: Training programs for 1 mile, 2 mile, 5K, and 1.5 mile runs are detailed in this book. There is also information on race-specific information in nutrition, mental toughness and running form. Also included are some very accurate prediction tests that allow you to tell what a realistic goal is. This book has been used effectively by those who are stuck in a performance rut at 10K or longer events. By training and racing faster, you can improve running efficiency and your tolerance for waste products, like lactic acid.

The stick

This massage tool can help the muscles recover quicker. It will often speed up the recovery of muscle injuries or Ilio-Tibial Band injuries (on the outside of the upper leg, between knee and hip). This type of device can warm up the leg muscles and reduce the aggravation of sore muscles and tendons. By promoting blood flow during and after a massage, muscle recovery time is reduced.

To use "the stick" on the calf muscle (most important in running), start each stroke at the achilles tendon and roll up the leg toward the knee. Gently roll back to the origin and continue, repeatedly. For the first 5 minutes a gentle rolling motion will bring additional blood flow to the area. As you gradually increase the pressure on the calf during an "up" stroke, you'll usually find some knots or sore places in the muscles. Concentrate on these as you roll over them again and again, gradually breaking up the tightness. See *www.RunInjuryFree.com* for more info on this.

Foam roller—self massage for I-T Band, Hip, etc.

This cylinder of dense foam is about 6 inches in diameter and about one foot long. I've not seen any mode of treatment for Ilio-Tibial band injury that has been more effective. For best effect, put the roller on the floor, and lie on your side so that the irritated I-T band area is on top of the roller. As your body weight presses down on the roller, roll up and down on the area of the leg you want to treat. Roll gently for 2-3 minutes and then apply more pressure as desired. This is actually a deep tissue massage that you can perform on yourself. For I-T band, I recommend rolling it before and after running. See *www.RunInjuryFree.com* for more info on this product.

Cryo-Cup—best tool for ice massage

Rubbing with a chunk of ice on a sore area (when near the skin) is very powerful therapy. I know of hundreds of cases of achilles tendon problems that have been healed by this method. The Cryo-Cup is a very convenient device for ice massage. The plastic cup has a plastic ring that sits on top of it. Fill it up with water and then freeze. When you have an ache or pain that is close to the skin, take the product out of the freezer, pour warm water over the outside of the cup to release it, and hold onto the plastic handle like an ice "popsicle." Rub constantly up and down the affected area for about 15 minutes, until the tendon is numb. When finished, fill the cup and place in the freezer. In my experience, rubbing with a plastic bag of ice—or a frozen gel product—does no good at all.

"You Can Do It" motivational audio CD

Put this in your car player as you drive to your run. You'll be motivated by the stories as you learn the strategies and methods that have allowed runners to deal with the negative messages of the left side of the brain—and pushed to their potential.

Endurox excel

Many runners over 50 years old have told me that they have noticed a significantly faster muscle rebound when using this product. An hour before a long or hard workout, I take two of these Excel pills. Among the anti-oxidants is the active ingredient from gensing: ciwega. Research has shown that recovery time is reduced when this product is taken. I also use it when my legs have been more tired than usual for 2-3 days in a row.

Accelerade

This sports drink has a patented formula shown to improve recovery. Drinking it before and after prolonged, dehydrating workouts also helps to improve hydration. I recommend having a half-gallon container of Accelerade in the refrigerator. Drink 4-8 oz every 1-2 hours, throughout the day. The best time to "top off" your fluid levels is within 24 hours before a long run. The prime time for replacing fluids is during the 24 hour period after a long run. Many runners have 32 oz in a thermos for sipping during walk breaks in a prolonged speed training session. I suggest adding about 25% more water than recommended.

Research has also shown that drinking Accelerade about 30 min before running can get the body's startup fuel (glycogen) activated more effectively, and may conserve the limited supply of this crucial fuel.

Endurox R4

This product has almost "cult following" status among runners. In fact, the research shows that the 4-1 ratio of carbohydrate to protein helps to reload the muscle glycogen more quickly (when consumed within 30 min of the finish of a hard or long workout). This means that the muscles feel bouncy and ready to do what you can do, sooner. There are other anti-oxidants in R4 that speed recovery.

Jeff Galloway's Training Journal

Some type of journal is recommended to organize and track your training plan. Jeff Galloway's Training Journal can be ordered from *www.JeffGalloway.com*, autographed. It simplifies the process, with places to fill in information for each day. There is also space for recording the unexpected thoughts and experiences that make so many runs come alive again as we read them.

Your journal allows you to take control of the organization of your training components. As you plan ahead, and then compare notes afterward, you are empowered to learn from your experience, and make positive changes.

Galloway PC Coach—interactive software

This software will not only set up a marathon training program, it will help you to stay on track. As you log in, you're told if your training is not what it should be for that day. Sort through various training components quickly, and often find reasons why you are tired or have more aches and pains.

Vitamins

I now believe that most runners need a good vitamin to boost the immune system and resist infection. There is some evidence that getting the proper vitamin mix can also speed recovery. The vitamin line I use is called Cooper Complete. Dr. Kenneth Cooper (founder of the Cooper Clinic and the Aerobics Institute), is behind this product. In the process of compiling the most formidable body of research on exercise and long-term health I've seen anywhere, he found that certain vitamins play important roles. For more information, see *www.coopercomplete.com*.

Buffered salt tablets—to reduce cramping

If your muscles cramp on long or hard runs because of salt depletion, this type of product may help. The buffered sodium and potassium tablets get into the system more quickly. Be sure to ask your doctor if this product is OK for you (those with high blood pressure, especially). If you are taking a statin drug for cholesterol, and are cramping, it is doubtful that this will help. Ask your doctor about adjusting the medication before long runs.

Prime Training

Elements

The following ingredients are described earlier in this book. They are like components in a sound system, which, when blended together create a wonderful sound that is greater than the sum of its parts. Please don't try to combine two or more of these—unless they are listed that way on the schedule. For example, you can do acceleration-gliders and cadence drills as a warm-up before speed or hill sessions. But if you try to accelerate in any way, during a long run, you will increase recovery time, and may injure yourself.

Long runs: Run these very slowly—at least 2 min/mi slower than you could run in a marathon as predicted by your "Magic Mile." Put in the walk breaks that are suggested in the Run-Walk-Run ™ chapter in this book. You cannot go too slowly on long runs. Slower long runs build the same endurance as fast long runs, with little or no risk of injury or burnout.

Drills: Cadence drills (CD) and acceleration gliders (Acg). These easy exercises teach your body to improve form as you improve running mechanics. They are not exhausting. Most runners say they energize an average run. Doing each of these drills once a week will improve speed and running efficiency.

"Magic Mile" Time Trials (TT or MM)

- Go to a track, or other accurately measured course.
- Warm up by walking for 5 minutes, then running 1 minute and walking 1 minute. Jog an easy 800 meter (half mile or two laps around a track).
- Do 4 cadence drills (CD) and 4 acceleration gliders. These are listed in the "Drills" chapter.
- Walk for 3-4 minutes.
- Run the 1 mile TT—a hard effort. Follow the walk break suggestions in the "Predicting Performance" chapter.
- In your first race, don't run all-out from the start. Ease into your pace after the first third of the distance. On each successive MM or TT, try to beat the time you ran in the previous one.
- Warm down by reversing the warm-up.
- A school track is the best venue. Don't use a treadmill because they tend to be notoriously un-calibrated and often tell you that you ran farther or faster than you really did. Run the first lap slightly slower than you think you can average. Take a short walk break as noted in the walk break suggestions. It is OK to be huffing and puffing on the last lap. If you are slowing down on the last lap, start a little slower on the next one. When you finish, you should feel like you couldn't run more than half a lap farther at that pace (if that).

Speed: A gradual increase in speed training can prepare you for the realistic goal of your choice. See the "Mature and Faster" section of this book.

Tempo or pace segments: These are segments which are run at your goal race pace, in the middle of short runs (not to be done on long runs). Run at race pace, taking the walk breaks as you plan to take them in the race. This is like a dress rehearsal for race day. By doing this exactly as you plan to do in your race, all of your performance systems get ready for the big day.
- Warm up with 5 min of walking, then 10 min of easy running and walking.
- Time yourself for a segment that is between half a mile and 2 miles.
- Run at your goal pace.
- Insert walk breaks as you plan to do so in the race.
- Do 1-3 miles of these segments.
- Don't do them if your legs are too tired.
- Reverse the warm-up as a warm down.

Track distances:
400 meters is one lap around a track, approximately a quarter mile.
800 meters is approximately half a mile, or two laps around a track.
1 mile is 4 laps around a track, within a few yards.

Advisors:

John Cantwell, M.D.
Diana Twiggs, M.D.
Steve Miller, M.D.
Tom Adair
Ruth Parker, M.D.
Julie Gazmararian, PhD MPH
Perry Julian, DPN
David Hannaford, DPN
Nancy Clark, MS, RD
Todd Whitthorne

Photo & Illustration Credits

Cover Photo: imago
Cover Design: Sabine Groten
Inside Photos: Polar Electro
                   Howell Kiser
                   Gregory Sheats
                   getty images/Digital Vision

Jeff Galloway: America´s No. 1 Running Book Author

Jeff Galloway
Running – Getting Started

3rd edition
ISBN: 9781841262420
$ 16.95 US / $ 29.95 AUS
£ 12.95 UK/€ 16.95

Jeff & Barbara Galloway
Women's Complete Guide to Running

2nd edition
ISBN: 9781841262055
$ 16.95 US / $ 29.95 AUS
£ 12.95 UK/€ 16.95

Jeff Galloway
Galloway's 5k and 10k Running

ISBN: 9781841262192
$ 16.95 US / $ 29.95 AUS
£ 12.95 UK/€ 16.95

Jeff Galloway
Running – A Year Round Plan

ISBN: 9781841261690
$ 17.95 US / $ 29.95 AUS
£ 14.95 UK/€ 16.95

Jeff Galloway
Running – Testing Yourself

2nd edition
ISBN: 9781841261676
$ 14.95 US / $ 29.95 AUS
£ 12.95 UK/€ 16.95

Jeff & Barbara Galloway
Running & Fat Burning for Women

2nd edition
ISBN: 9781841262437
$ 17.95 US / $ 32.95 AUS
£ 14.95 UK/€ 16.95

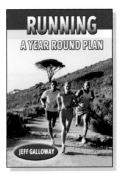

Jeff Galloway
Half-Marathon – You Can Do It

3rd edition
ISBN: 9781841261904
$ 16.95 US / $ 29.95 AUS
£ 12.95 UK/€ 16.95

Jeff Galloway
Galloway's Marathon FAQ

ISBN: 9781841262666
$ 17.95 US / $ 29.95 AUS
£ 12.95 UK/€ 16.95

Galloway/Hannaford
Running Injuries Treatment and Prevention

ISBN 9781841262840
$ 16.95 US / $ 29.95 AUS
£ 12.95 UK/€ 16.95

The Sports Publisher

MEYER & MEYER Sport | www.m-m-sports.com
sales@m-m-sports.com

MEYER & MEYER SPORT